AESOP'S COLLEGE

AESOP'S COLLEGE

by

PHIL ADAMO

BOOKS

Copyright © 2023 Phillip C. Adamo

Published by Split Infinitive Books, LLC
Minneapolis, MN 55407

All rights reserved. No part of this publication may be reproduced, distributed, or transmitted in any form or by any means, including photocopying, recording, or other electronic or mechanical methods, without the prior written permission of the publisher, except in the case of brief quotations embodied in critical reviews and certain other noncommercial uses permitted by copyright law.

This is a work of fiction. Names, characters, places, and incidents are either the product of the author's imagination or are used fictitiously, and any resemblance to events, locations, persons or animals, living or dead, business establishments, events or locales, is entirely coincidental.

Printed in the United States of America.

ISBN-13: 978-1-7327793-1-0

For Alison

I took the myths of Aesop, which I had at hand and knew, and turned into verse the first I came upon.

> — Plato, *The Phaedo* (4th century BC)

The question is not, "Can [animals] reason?" nor, "Can they talk?" but, "Can they suffer?"

> — Jeremy Bentham, *An Introduction to the Principles of Morals and Legislation* (1780)

Lepus cerebrum—Mens testudo"
(Hare brain—turtle mind.)

> — Latin motto of Aesop College

CHAPTER 1

"Mungojerrie?"

The Provost spoke the name slowly and with concern as she cradled the phone between her picnic shoulder and what, under different circumstances, might have made a very nice silk purse.

"Yes, yes," she continued. "Yes, I know the poem ... In class? ... Out loud? ... Damn."

She hung up the phone and spun around in her Herman Miller Aeron chair. The rotary motion sent gentle air currents through the chair's patented, elastomeric fabric, keeping the Provost's legs and back cool. Since her legs didn't reach the ground, it took three spins before she could stop the chair facing the bookshelf behind her desk, where she pulled a slim volume off the middle shelf. The Provost had been a physics professor before going into administration, but she had become obsessed with the musical *Cats* while still an undergraduate, so she knew this collection of poems very well. Hers was a first edition, published in 1939, with illustrations by the author himself. The drawings were not sophisticated, but to her mind they added a charm to the book that was indisputable. The orange dustjacket bore an ink rendering of a mustachioed man in a high collar and bowler hat holding a ladder, apparently assisting several cats as they made their escape over a brick wall. The title and the

2 Adamo

"Mungojerrie?" The Provost spoke the name slowly.

author's name were printed in a simple but neat hand: T.S. Elliot, *Old Possum's Book of Practical Cats*.

"Elliot," the Provost said laughing, which for her always sounded more like snorting. With her flat, damp snout, she opened the book and turned the pages, paying little attention to the brittle crackling of the tea-colored paper, until she reached the opening lines of the poem.

"Mungojerrie and Rumpleteazer, bada-BOP-ba-BOP-bada-BAda-ba-DOP."

The Provost had always been able to read—at least she could not remember a time when she couldn't—but without opposable thumbs, turning the pages of books was difficult. She much preferred reading works on her computer. A mouse is much easier to manipulate, she thought to herself and clucked her tongue. She pressed the intercom button with a cloven hoof and shouted orders to her administrative assistant, a white, former lab rat just outside her office.

"Mrs. Pilfer," she said, "have Professor Socks come to my office."

"Right away, Provost Hamhock," Pilfer replied.

The Provost leaned back in her Herman Miller Aeron chair as far as it would lean and reminisced about the first time she met Socks.

It was Reinvention Day. "Reinvention" was the name the human students had given to their liberation of the animals, since it caused both animals and humans to reinvent their relationship to one another.

Gullinburst Hamhock, who would later become Provost of Aesop College, walked across the quad and absorbed the celebration. Humans and animals of all kinds had come together. There were squirrels, of course, who had always lived in the quad, but they were more interested in the rubbish bins and whatever handouts the students might offer than anything to do with academics or the inner workings of the college. The quad was no stranger to dogs, who every afternoon romped and fetched sticks and caught flying disks at the behest of their humans. Now the dogs ran off leash, willy-nilly, while cats, who once sat in windows observing the dogs with disdain, sauntered across the freshly mown lawn. Comfort rabbits zig-zagged through the feet of their human students, trying to avoid the cats' gaze. Lab rats huddled along the windowsills of Reinvention Hall, which used to be called Invention Hall, because it housed the sciences. The word "INVENTION" was chiseled *au naturel* into the yellow granite lintel above the door. A student had colored in all the letters with bright red paint, then painted the prefix RE- in front of the word, so it looked something like this:

RE **INVENTION**

A four-foot ball python named Nora eyed the rats from the crux of two branches in an elm tree. Gullinburst Hamhock's hams were too large for her to balance on a ledge. She certainly couldn't climb a tree, so she found a spot in front of the administration building, where some of the students had set up a makeshift platform and microphone. There she had the best view of whatever was going to happen next. Hamhock looked out over the interspecies gathering in the quad. At least no one is being eaten, she thought.

J. "Dusty" Adams, human president of what at that time was known as McDonald College, approached the platform. He was tall and willowy, with thinning hair and a black pencil moustache that resembled a busy caterpillar. As Adams adjusted the microphone, audio feedback filled the quad with a piercing sound that startled some of the animals, especially the rabbits, who froze in place, ears erect. A human student assigned to the A.V. department fiddled with the volume, but when Adams returned to the mic, the same screeching poured forth. This time, dogs began to howl, while the rabbits scattered and tried to hide as best they could under the deep groundcover at the foot of the ivy-covered buildings. The human A.V. student adjusted more knobs on his console then hurried to the platform to examine the mic. As soon as the student touched the mic, the squealing feedback stopped, but when he took his hand away and offered the mic to Adams, the squealing returned. Touch. No squealing. Remove hand. Squealing. This went on for two or three rounds as all the animals and humans looked on, until finally the feedback was replaced by cackling. A crow named Lucifer, who had been imitating the audio feedback for his own amusement, nearly fell out of a tree from laughter.

President Adams looked sternly at the crow, waved a dismissive hand, and took the microphone again.

"My fellow Mackies," he said. "Faculty, staff, students, and, if I may ... animals. This is an historic day for McDonald College. No less historic than that day in 1822 when Old Angus McDonald left Scotland for America to found this great school ... *McDonald* College ..."

It was the same speech that Adams gave at every opening convocation, at every commencement exercise, at every fundraising dinner.

"McDonald has always reinvented itself. We were one of the first colleges in America to go co-ed. When enrollments were down during World War II because so many men had joined the fight against the Nazis, we encouraged women to come to McDonald ..."

Hamhock saw human students near the platform roll their eyes and feign yawning. Get on with it, they seemed to be saying.

"And during the civil rights movement, when Congress mandated that federal education dollars should follow students of color to private schools, we opened our doors to blacks and Latinos ..."

"LatinX!" a human student shouted from the far end of the quad.

"LatinX?" the president stuttered and turned to one of his aides, who had vetted his speech. "Is that plural? I thought LatinX was supposed to cover the full range of genders, but is it plural, too? What do we do if there's a whole group of LatinXes?" The aide pointed back at the script and nodded toward the audience, indicating that the president should not lose focus.

"Our founders and predecessors," Adams continued, "did not accept the received wisdom of their day but were innovators in thought and deed. They were marginalized white men who took risks to make the world a better place. And ever since, McDonald has sought out the marginalized to increase enrollments, ahem … increase engagement with the wider world …"

Bees from a rooftop hive flew down into the quad to see what all the fuss was about, but their droning was no match for the droning of the president. Another ten minutes of blah, blah, blah and Adams invited the student body president to speak.

"… for which we were named the most LGBT-friendly campus in America, not to mention the QIA and the LMNOP. McDonald College has always been a place of reinvention, a place where students don't learn to change the world, but to reinvent it. And so, on this Reinvention Day, let me turn things over to your student body president, Liliana Carnevale."

A slight woman took to the platform. For all intents and purposes, she looked like a girl that a traditional mother and father would want as their daughter. She did not have a shaved head or tattoos or a nose ring—that last one would have been especially insulting to pigs and bulls, since they had long been forced to wear nose rings as a means of control.

"I'm Lili. With an 'I.' Well, two I's. I'm here to talk about my great awakening to animal rights. I'm a cis-gender, sixth-gen Italian-American, so, white, heterosexual female, and I can only speak from my positionality and intersectionality, which includes a life of practicing species-ism toward 99% of the world's sentient living creatures. Until now." The audience offered a host of approving sounds, from humans snapping their fingers (clapping might trigger fright or anxiety) to cats purring to rats making little squeaking noises. Hamhock, who had been Lili's comfort pig, sat up straight and looked admiringly at her one-time owner.

"I used to think that it was enough to be a vegan," Carnevale continued. "But that was before my eyes were opened to all the ways that humans have abused our fellow roommates in the great dormitory of life." She looked down at Hamhock and her eyes welled up.

"Most of you know Gullinburst Hamhock," she continued, gesturing for the pig to join her on the platform. "She was my comfort animal. No, no. There are so many things wrong with that sentence. First, I can't believe the name I gave you. As if it was even my right to assign you a name. Gullinburst! My childish obsession with Norse mythology gone cuckoo. No, not 'cuckoo.' That's anti-avian. Forgive me. Oh, Gullinburst! My feeble attempt to be 'cutesy' steals your dignity. I'm so ashamed. Can you ever forgive me?"

She took the mic from its stand and knelt down so she could address the pig at eye-level.

"And to call you *my* comfort animal, as if you were just a thing that I, or anyone, could own. And *comfort* animal? As if it was *your* job to comfort *me!*"

Lili related how stressful changing the world could be, especially while maintaining a 4.0 grade-point average and a complete intolerance for intolerance. Comfort animals alleviated that stress, filling in the gaps when students were unable to get parental nurturing via hourly video phone chats.

"Ridiculous!" said Lili. "There were other ways I could have comforted myself. That kind of thinking imposes a power relationship where there doesn't have to be one, puts humans above, and animals below. It's the last remnant of white, heterosexual male hegemony!" Lili threw her arms around Gullinburst's neck and began to cry.

"You talk," she said, gesturing to the pig. "It's condescending of me to talk for you. You talk."

In spite of the potential triggering effect, the humans in the crowd began a loud round of applause, amid shouts of "Hamhock! Hamhock!" It was difficult for Gullinburst to hold onto the mic—cloven hooves and all—and Lili didn't think it right to hold the mic on the pig's behalf (promoting an arrogant, able-ist agenda), so she re-attached the mic to its stand and adjusted this toward Gullinburst so that it was level with the pig's snout.

Hamhock had never spoken to a crowd before, much less a mixed crowd of animals and humans. She felt confident that she could communicate to her fellow mammals and even to the birds and reptiles, but Lili was the only human that she had ever conversed with, and that was quite different than giving a speech. She gave the mic a soft tap—something she had seen other speakers do—and cleared her throat.

"My fellow ... animals. For we are all animals, are we not?" Her diction was good, and her voice rang clear, with the neutral Midwestern accent preferred by broadcast journalists.

"We are all animals. Yet, as one of the great books tells us, some of us are more animal than others. There is a long history behind this way of thinking that we need not rehearse here." For a pig that had been called to speak on the spur of the moment, she was surprisingly poised, not to mention well-informed.

"Let me focus my remarks on language and all the ways that language harms our inter-species relationships. 'Wild animal.' 'Pet.' 'Owner.' 'Master!' Words have power and words such as these establish a power dynamic that ill serves any animal except humans. Consider the word 'pest,' which Mr. Webster defines as 'something prone to destructiveness; esp., a plant or animal detrimental to humans or human concerns (as agriculture or livestock production)' or 'one that pesters or annoys.' Raccoons foraging in garbage cans, rabbits and deer feeding in planted gardens, all are considered pests, although they are only following their instincts, their genetic destiny. Even a neighbor's dog who barks when a human is trying to sleep is called a pest. Any animal interfering with a human (even when that animal is another human) may be called a pest. It should be clear from these examples that the word has no relation to the animal's inherent qualities, but only to the animal's behavior in relation to what humans expect of it. The term is entirely humano-centric!"

Fingers snapping, squirrel cheeks clucking, rat paws scratching their approval.

"The list of vicious stereotypes assigned to animals is breathtaking and appalling. For centuries, humans have used animal terms to denigrate their fellow humans. A bat is a silly old woman, but a fox is a sexy young woman. A cat is a spiteful woman, but a cow is a woman who's fat—by whose standards? A chicken is a coward, though a hen is an overprotective mother and a cock is an overly proud man. A deer is just plain dumb, with its eyes in the headlights. The word dog has any number of applications: nasty dog, lazy dog, bitch! There are so many of these and I'm not even past the Ds."

"Donkeys are stubborn." A human student shouted from the audience. People booed, even though it was clear that he was just offering an example of the offensive language that Hamhock was talking about.

"No, no," Hamhock said. "Let's hear more examples."

"Shy as a mouse," one of the rats on the windowsill shouted.

"Smart as a beagle," a beagle yelled out, which brought giggles and many confused looks.

"Hung like a horse," a frat boy standing under the elm tree offered up and laughed to the other frat boys around him, seeking their approval. Nora the python, perched above the frat boy's head, let her tail slip off the branch and brush the back of the frat boy's neck causing him to "squeal like a pig," which made every human and animal in his immediate vicinity laugh out loud.

"Finally," Hamhock continued, "words like 'owner' and 'master.' Dog owner, cat owner, pet owner. To own something is to consider it property, but property is inanimate, a house, a car. Animals cannot be inanimate. It's in their name! Animal, from the Latin *animus*, 'breath', which later evolves into the idea of the soul. God breathing life into Adam, and all that. As sentient beings, animals cannot be owned any more than humans can be owned, although the history of humanity is a long record of humans owning other humans, and this never turns out well."

Hamhock elegantly told the story of comfort animals coming to McDonald College. At first, their numbers were limited to dogs and rabbits, but it was quickly expanded to cats, then snakes, lizards, canaries, goldfish, rats, ferrets, sugar gliders, frogs, and eventually pigs. The human-led administration drew the line at dwarf horses. All of this was well and good, and the now-destressed students could focus on learning stuff that would help them reinvent the world. Then one day, Lili Carnevale, the human student for whom Hamhock provided comfort, realized that all these comfort animals were also a part of the world. Didn't student use of comfort animals constitute exploitation of sentient beings?

"This created a paradox," Hamhock explained, "that eventually became too much to bear—though I do not mean any disrespect to bears (*Ursidae*) by using the homophonic verb. Perhaps it's best to say that McDonald's students found this paradox between the use of comfort animals and their exploitation a difficult burden. Over the last several months, great debates have taken place, in the classrooms and in the quad, that have brought us to this historic moment. The human students have finally realized that animals and humans are equals."

Snap. Chirp. Purr. Croak. Howl. As the various sounds of approval washed over Gullinburst Hamhock, the world around her seemed to slow down and her eyes locked on the one sentient being who was not chirping or howling, and he certainly was not purring. It was Socks, the mysterious, blue merle border collie.

She had never met Socks, though she had often seen him in the quad. Socks was a campus dog, not a comfort dog. He slept in a storm drain when the weather was good, and when the weather turned bad, he snuck into the library through a basement window and slept among the stacks. This explained his access to the many books Hamhock had witnessed him reading. Long before he joined the faculty, Socks could be found giving lectures or conducting seminars from his storm drain, with dozens of animals gathered around the opening listening to him hold forth on topics as diverse as Kant's categorical imperative and Shakespeare's sonnets. He never chased Frisbees, though according to one rumor he had been a champion in agility, fly ball, and dock diving. No. Socks read. Everything.

Socks's polychromatic eyes (one blue, one brown) met Hamhock's eyes. It wasn't love at first site or anything that one might call a romantic connection—in those days, inter-species relationships were possible, but still new—but there was an intellectual intensity, an electrical charge between the two of them that signaled they would either be great allies or great foes.

There was more speechifying about the plan to turn the college over to the animals: how they had been denied the benefits of education for too long, how truly inclusive society must include those who had feathers and scales, those with four legs and those with fangs. President Adams would step down and serve in an advisory role to the new president, a fox named Reynaldo Sourgrapes. The human faculty, weary of students so engaged in reinventing the world that they disengaged from academics, would retire as soon as the college could recruit suitable animal replacements. Although any animal could attend classes, it was decided that the student body would be made up mostly of cats. The feline demographic was the biggest and provided the best chance for a sustainable economic model. Cats preferred to be pampered, but they might be teachable.

Finally, animal students would give their school a new name, to signal its reinvention: Aesop College.

McDonald was old. It signaled a time when animals were but servants to their masters. Aesop was fresh, in spite of the name's antiquity. The animal characters in Aesop's stories were self-determining. Rather than having humans act upon their lives, they exercised agency and controlled their own destinies. They made their own decisions. And when they made mistakes, they were able to learn from them. Aesop. It was the perfect name for a new kind of college.

The speeches ended and the humans and animals began to disperse. Still, Hamhock and Socks held each other's gaze. Lili noticed how her pig … her former pig …oh, why this obsession with possessive pronouns? She must break herself of that habit. She noticed how Gullinburst, if she decided to stick with that name, was staring at Socks. Lili was a little afraid of dogs, but she wanted to make introductions if she could. It was only polite. She asked the president if he would help, if he knew the name of the border collie who was now sitting alone in a perfect "sit."

"Of course," Adams said, then turned to Sourgrapes in a whispered aside. "This one might make a good professor."

"Let's all go to meet him," Sourgrapes replied with a foxy grin.

The four of them (outgoing President Adams, incoming President Sourgrapes, Student Body President Liliana Carnevale, and soon-to-be Provost Hamhock) stepped down from the platform and walked toward Socks. As soon as he saw them coming, the dog lay down and assumed the most indifferent pose he could muster.

"Excuse me, Socks," the outgoing president said. "We've only met once before, but, of course, your reputation precedes you. Dusty Adams." He extended his hand expecting the border collie to respond with a well-executed "shake" or "paw," but Socks offered no response.

"Uh, this is Reynaldo Sourgrapes, the new, uh, incoming, mmm, founding president of Aesop College. I'm sure he'll want to talk to you about, perhaps, joining the faculty." Still no response, though Socks did briefly lick his testicles.

"Uh, any chance you might be interested? Anything we could do to sweeten the deal? Heh-heh."

"Yes," Socks said. He momentarily locked eyes with the fox, then looked up at the outgoing, human president. "Stand a little out of my sun."

"Stand a little out of my sun." The distant memory of that day brought a smile to Hamhock's moon-shaped mug. That was five years ago.

Since then, Socks had indeed joined the faculty. And she, Gullinburst Hamhock, had risen through the ranks of that faculty to become the Provost. Aesop College had grown in reputation. Some critics claimed that McDonald's graduation rate had set such a low bar that Aesop's standing could only go up. Cats did matriculate and some of them made decent students. The outlook was stable, though there was an ongoing problem with retention.

This was why episodes like "the Mungojerrie incident" were so dangerous. It upset the cats and if enough of them got so upset that they left the college, it could spell financial ruin.

The intercom on her desk buzzed and the voice of Mrs. Pilfer squawked through.

"Professor Socks," she said.

"Send him in."

Chapter 2

Mrs. Pilfer's pink eyes squinted down at Socks. She didn't trust him. It was more than the usual distrust between predator and prey. This border collie was too smart for his own good. Everyone thought so, and she should know because one of her skills was lurking in the shadows and listening in on everyone's conversations. She had heard plenty of stories about Socks! She once witnessed a meeting between the border collie and the human president, Adams, who was trying his best to win the dog over with what he believed to be his human charm.

"You know," Adams said, attempting to blush, "if I weren't myself … a human, you know … I'd wish to be Socks."

The border collie cocked his head to the left. His ears were erect, except for the tips, which flopped forward. On most dogs this expression was ridiculously cute and signaled friendly curiosity. For Socks, it was a sign that you were about to be served a dog dish of his cynical wit.

"If I weren't Socks," he said, "and especially if I were you, a human, I too would wish to be Socks."

What an ass! Mrs. Pilfer thought, then mentally apologized to all the donkeys of the world, even though she had never met one. Yet this was exactly the kind of intel the Provost had come to depend on Mrs. Pilfer to deliver.

Pilfer spent the early days of her life running mazes in the college psychology lab until the great events of Reinvention Day had set her free. She was thankful to have landed in the

What an ass! Mrs. Pilfer thought.

Provost's office, though she sometimes felt that the Provost treated her like ... well, she'd rather not say. Nonetheless, she was grateful for her position at the college. The job provided regular food, shelter, and medical coverage, which extended her lifespan threefold over that of her cousins, the *Rattus norvegicus*, or Norwegian rat, a.k.a. the common rat, the street rat, the sewer rat, water rat, wharf rat, Hanover rat, and Parisian rat—oo la la. And the Provost did seem appreciative whenever she was able to deliver detailed reports from all corners of the campus.

"You can't spell administrator," the Provost once said to her, "without R-A-T."

The border collie held her gaze.

Mrs. Pilfer could have simply gestured toward the door to allow the dog to enter the Provost's office. Instead, she scurried down the wire from the phone on her desk to the ground, raced across the floor, then jumped straight up to catch the door handle, which she held with all four paws as she allowed her weight to turn the handle and open the door. As it eased open, she spun around and blocked the dog's entrance, staring directly into his eyes. She had no intention of letting him walk in without formally announcing his presence in person. But seeing the rat on all fours, the dog read this as an invitation to play. Socks crouched down with his front legs, his rear end high in the air, tail wagging.

Oh, crap, Mrs. Pilfer wanted to think to herself, but before she could fully form that thought, they were off. Socks chased the poor rat over every inch of the Provost's office, under tables and across filing cabinets, up and down chairs. For every zig the rat offered, the dog parried with an appropriate zag. Her final move sent Pilfer across the Provost's desk. Socks pursued. Papers scattered like white parachutes from a field of dandelions gone to seed. Mrs. Pilfer ended on the Provost's head, peeking out from between both ears. Socks, legs splayed on the desk, looked up at the rat. The Provost leaned forward until her wet snout touched the dog's wet nose.

"Professor Socks," announced Mrs. Pilfer, attempting to regain some sense of decorum.

"I see that," said Provost Hamhock.

Exhausted by these efforts, Pilfer cautiously crawled down the Provost's back, then exited the office performing ritual obeisance as she left, bowing her head to touch the ground between her front paws as her tail beat out a slow metronomic dance of retreat.

Socks, still lying comfortably on the Provost's desk, unrolled his tongue and began to pant through an adrenaline-charged smile.

Just before this homage to Tom and Jerry disrupted her office, Hamhock had momentarily set aside *Old Possum's Book of Practical Cats* and returned to her review of Isaac Newton's *Principia Mathematica*. She sat in awe that Newton had invented calculus (Leibniz be damned!) in order to interpret and understand the movement of the heavens. A favorite hobby, in her few spare minutes of each day, was checking Newton's proofs in long form. Now all of her paper-and-pencil practice had been scattered to the four winds, replaced by 50 pounds of silky-haired intellect and folly.

"Get. Off. My. Desk," she said.

"Come down to the ground with us four-leggers, and I will."

Sitting in the Herman Miller Aeron chair, although it was only nineteen inches off the ground, added dignity to the Provost's position. It also sent a message about pecking order that all the animals understood, though not all of the animals respected. The one thing that deflated any dignity of her office was watching the Gloucester Old Spots pig mounting or dismounting the chair, with its wheeled legs and its spinning seat. Hamhock preferred to be already seated before her meetings began. She absolutely hated coming down to Socks's level (in every way), but she knew the dog would not get off her desk unless she dismounted. The Provost rocked and wobbled back and forth on her ham, trying to shift her center of gravity. She could manage the seat's spinning but had no control over the wheels on the chair's feet. When she finally reached escape velocity, the action of her dismount caused a reaction in the chair, confirming Newton's third law of motion as it shot across the room.

The border collie jumped off the desk and herded the pig toward a large round rug in the center of the office. For her part, the Provost let him believe that he was the one doing the herding. On her way to the rug, Hamhock retrieved the book of Elliot's poems, which had been knocked to the ground during the chase scene. Socks circled a spot on the rug and settled in. Hamhock laid the book down in front of him and plopped her hams down as well. They sat eye to eye. In spite of the dog's disruptive entrance, Hamhock hoped to ease Socks into the difficult discussion they were about to have.

"How are you doing this semester?" she asked.

"Dog tired!" he replied.

"Do you mind not using these offensive clichés?"

"Do you mind not pussyfooting around? Besides, as a dog, I should be allowed to say 'dog tired,' especially if I'm using it to describe myself."

"You do look a bit dog-eared."

"And how about you? Happy as a pig in sh—"

"Watch it!"

He smiled and shook his head. Reaching across the carpet, she extended her petittoe and pushed the collection of Elliot's poems closer to Socks.

"How's the course reading going?"

"Pearls before swine," he said, unable to resist sneaking in one last jab. The Provost did not laugh at this one.

"Your students are all cats," she said sternly, "not swine. I've heard that they're upset about the reading."

This was Hamhock's method of indirect communication. 'I've heard that …' or, 'What do you think about …'. But Socks was on to her.

"I hear they're concerned about your use of the M-word," she said.

"Which one? Elliot uses lots of words that start with M."

"You know full well which one."

"Look," Socks said. His face adopted that expression he always got when he had to explain something so obvious, especially to someone so bright. "We're studying the great twentieth-century poets, Elliot among them. But you can't make a bunch of cats jump into the deep end with 'April is the blah bah blah desire.' So, I soften up their palates with the *Practical Book of Cats*. Get them to like old Thomas Stearns' style through this silly little book, and only then hit them with *The Waste Land*."

"That's a perfectly reasonable pedagogical approach," the Provost said. "But how do you handle the hurtful words in the text? Specifically, … 'Mungojerrie.'"

"Ah, the swallows have arrived at Capistrano."

"Did you say the word? Out loud?"

"It's in the text. It *starts* the text. Out loud? Yes, of course I read it out loud. It's poetry for dog's sake. How else should it be read?"

Expecting resistance, the Provost took her time before she continued.

"You realize this has upset the students."

"They're cats. 'Upset' is their resting state."

"This is serious."

"No. Sirius is the dog star, the brightest in the sky, just to the left of Orion's Belt.

"Socks!"

"I read the passage. I used the word," Socks said. He then described the range of student reactions. Some of the cats yammered when they heard it. Others hissed. Some opened their mouths wide and stretched out their tongues. Others lowered their heads and flattened their ears. All of them had widened pupils. Some of them blinked rapidly.

"I listened to their various opinions," Socks concluded. "I acknowledged their opinions but pursued a line of inquiry that I thought was relevant."

"You acknowledged their opinions, but what about their feelings?" Hamhock asked.

"What's the difference between the two?"

"I don't mean the way opinions are offered using such expressions as 'I feel that dog collar doesn't complement your coat.' I mean feelings, as in 'you hurt me by saying words that are meant to hurt.'"

"Honestly," Socks said. "What do their feelings have to do with anything? We're here to follow intellectual pursuits."

"Unfortunately," the Provost snorted, "their feelings are important. You must realize that you can't teach a student, especially a cat, if they feel that you've insulted or injured them in some way."

"But that's not—"

The Provost held up her trotter and cut him off.

"There's a video," she said.

"Beg pardon?"

"A video," she repeated. "One of the cats was wearing a camera around her neck and filmed the class. Apparently, it's all the rage these days."

In fact, almost all the cats and many of the other animals lived lives that were cultivated entirely online. A platform called Pintercat displayed thousands of photographs of the meals that cats were about to eat. They showed mushy canned food in every shade from pink to brown, or dry kibble in the shape of tiny fish, piled into dishes that were metal or plastic or ceramic, in all colors. Some of the bowls were close to the ground with non-skid rubber pads on the bottom, others were elevated so the cat wouldn't have to stoop to feed. Some of the bowls refilled themselves, either through electric dispensers or mechanical levers the cats could control themselves. Some had images of a cat's face in the bottom that could only be seen after all the food had been eaten. Others had stencils of fish skeletons or paw prints etched around the sides, while others had clever sayings like "Purr" and "Meow." Priceless.

These were just the still photos. There were also countless videos containing every possible scenario. They showed cats chasing their own tails, cats jumping in and out of paper bags, cats playing the piano, watching TV, looking out the window studying birds, or sometimes ghosts that only they could see. There were cats encountering other cats and cats encountering other species: rabbits, raccoons, chickens, human babies. Sometimes these encounters ended with the cat abruptly batting with their claws at the other animal's nose, but more often it showed the cats making unlikely alliances with the non-cats, evoking surprise and pleasure in the viewer.

As if the thousands of hours of cat videos, available on line 24/7, were not enough, cities across the country featured cat video festivals that played in auditoriums and baseball parks and were carefully curated by museum professionals.

There were even celebrity cats, like Frumpy Cat, whose only claim to fame was that his resting face consisted of bulging eyes and a downturned mouth that rendered an expression of disgust or anger, though who knew what the cat was really feeling inside. When Frumpy Cat died, as even cats must do, humans posted their condolences online to Fakebook and Flitter and some human TV news outlets ran the story, ironically, in the "human interest" segments of their broadcasts. Most cats found Frumpy Cat to be a bit of a publicity hound and held him in disdain, but others recognized that he was merely a victim of the culture in which he lived.

In such a culture, it was inevitable that the cats should start to record themselves. They began to wear tiny cameras around their necks so that every detail of their lives could be captured. As natural-born hunters, their very essence was to capture.

This is how the video of Socks's class came into being. One of the cats in his class, it wasn't clear which one, had been wearing a VidPro Constant Companion Camera attached to their collar. It was so small it resembled a vaccination tag (never say "dog tag"), and it could record up to ten hours of video before it had to be downloaded then uploaded to another platform, in this case, ZooTube. Socks looked back and forth from the computer screen to the Provost.

"Shall I show you?" the Provost asked.

With a look of resignation on his face, Socks nodded. Hamhock rose from the rug in the middle of her office and hoisted her front half onto her desk. Socks joined her, balancing on his hind legs to get a better view of the computer. The Provost grabbed the electronic mouse with her trotter and navigated to the ZooTube page where the video had already been uploaded. Socks immediately bristled at its title.

****WARNING: SPECIES SLUR INCIDENT****
ANTI-CAT-ITE PROFESSOR DEFENDS USE OF
THE M-WORD!

"What?! I never defended—"

"Let's just watch," the Provost said.

The video offered a paw-held point of view, mostly of Socks, but occasionally panning the classroom for reactions from the feline students. It sometimes jerked about, trying to capture student replies in a back and forth that lasted about seven minutes. It opened with a video version of Socks, standing in front of the classroom, reciting the Elliot poem: "Mungojerrie and Rumpleteazer ..."

The cats off camera gasped, yowled, and caterwauled. As the frame turned toward them, some of the cats blinked repeatedly, stretched their mouths, and flattened their ears, just as Socks had described. Some looked away, over their right shoulders. Two or three hid under their desks. A grey Persian named Magda made little chirrup sounds and licked her nose and fur for self-comfort. Several of the cats, with ears pointed outward, eyes wide and pupils dilated, hunched down as if prepared to pounce. The tension in the room rivaled that moment when a rabbit realizes a hawk is swooping down for them and they must decide in which direction to run.

"Okay," the Socks in the video said. "It seems this has struck a nerve. I need to ask you all a question." He paused, trying to make eye contact with each of the cats individually. "In a classroom," he continued, "quoting from an author's work, was it okay to say the word 'Mungojerrie' if the author had written it that way?" Quiet. Was this shock? Silent rage? Had they become so offended that they tuned out? He continued. "Wasn't substituting the euphemistic phrase 'the M-word' for Mungojerrie, in fact, a disservice to T.S. Elliot's great poetry?"

A striped tabby named Robespierre—who ironically had a mark on his forehead that resembled the letter M—was the first to speak.

"That word offends me," said Robespierre. "It makes me feel unsafe. As a cat who bears the mark of M, I've experienced life threatening situations, including attacks by dogs! That word triggers me. It feels like an assault."

A Siamese cat named Chiffon, friends with Robespierre, spoke next. "If the word makes Robespierre uncomfortable," she said, "then I don't think the word should be said."

A battered black cat with a thick white stripe down his chest brought up the question of context. "Lots of cats use the word. Like alley cats when they're rummaging through the trash and talking trash to each other. That seems to be okay."

"Yes," Chiffon said, "but that's an example of the oppressed species reclaiming the anti-cat-ite word to give it less power."

"I've never understood how that works," said an orange longhair. "If they can use it, why can't I?"

"Because you're not an alley cat." Chiffon said. "You live in a nice dorm room with a human and so you have privilege. For you to use that word would be abusing your power."

"It's like calling someone 'catty,'" Magda offered, still grooming herself.

"It's much worse!" the other cats hissed.

A lithe, ruddy Abyssinian named Cleopatra jumped down from the desk where she'd been perched and began to rub up against the legs of a chair.

"My history is very different from these domestic cats," she said. "Even though I've had people use the M-word to try to insult me or hurt my feelings, the word doesn't have the same impact on me as it does for cats who have always lived in this country. Still, I see why they find it offensive and I prefer not to say it."

The camera jerked back around to the front of the room as Socks jumped back into the conversation.

"So, if I've understood you correctly, you all prefer never to say the word out loud, even though the poet has written it that way. And instead we should read the line as 'M-word and Rumpleteazer—'"

"I don't like 'Rumpleteazer,'" said a smoke-colored Devon Rex from underneath one of the desks. It was Tiny Tim, who had just grown out of kitten-hood and was attending his first college class. "Rumple sounds like rumpled or messy and that's just rude. Cats are the cleanest mammals on the planet and to make fun of them like that isn't nice. And 'teaser'! Well, teasing is mean and leads to bullying and bullying shouldn't be done because it isn't nice."

"Don't say 'bullying,'" Chiffon said. "It's disrespectful to bulls."

"The word bullying doesn't have anything to do with bulls," Socks corrected. "In fact, the word bully used to be positive. Like when the Brits say, 'Bully for you, old chap.'"

"Did he just do a British accent?" a feline voice off camera asked.

"Cultural appropriation!" another yowled.

"No. no," another mewed. "Border collies are British so it's okay if he does the accent. At least I think it's okay."

The camera jerked back and forth but comments were coming too quickly to land and focus on any individual speaker. Sock tried to regain control of the classroom.

"Okay. If I've got this right, instead of accurately quoting the verse, written by one of the greatest human poets of the twentieth century, we're going to read it as follows: 'M-word and R-word were a very notorious couple of cats.' Yes?"

Yes, the cats purred, content that they had seemingly gotten their point across.

"I can only speak for myself," Robespierre said, "but I prefer that approach rather than hearing the actual word ever again." More collective purring, which one could hear growing louder on the video.

"Well, I think that's ridiculous," Socks said after a few seconds. "But if it means we can continue discussing Elliot's work, then I suppose it will have to do."

That's where the video ended.

Socks cocked his head, remembering the classroom exchange and trying to understand why this should be posted to ZooTube.

"Then there are the comments," the Provost said.

"Comments?"

"Oh, yes," the Provost added. "The entire internet, one of the greatest human inventions since soy-based bacon substitutes, is fueled by comments and angry responses to those comments and angry responses to those angry responses, paper bullets of the brain mixing it up in the outrage industrial complex. Look. Your video has over 500 views."

"500? The class only ended an hour ago!"

Socks began to read the comments but didn't get far before he had to stop. They were too painful.

"He looks like that dog from the Babe movie. *That* guy was an asshole to Babe; didn't believe a pig was smart enough to herd sheep. Hah!"

"This pisses me off so much, he always tries to act so woke, what a disappointment to Aesop College, seriously."

"you needa get your dog-ass profs in check."

"He's skeered. It's Going Down!"

"#Socks should quit"

One commenter asked if the students had gotten permission to film.

"Fuck his permission," said another commenter. "This needs to be heard."

Another commenter posted a link to an online petition that called on Aesop College to "take action and punish Socks." Among the complaints listed in the petition was the claim that "Even after the incident, Socks still doesn't seem to grasp what the issue is. Says he's 'just spicing up the text.'" Although the phrase appeared in quotes, Socks had never uttered it, nor anything to that effect. The facts don't seem to matter, he thought. Very depressing.

"Right then," Hamhock said. "Let's get to work on your apology so we can put this behind us."

"Apology?"

"Well, yes. You'll have to say you're sorry, since you hurt the students' feelings and you need to be sure to own your wrongdoing and say something about how you plan to change your ways in the future."

"But I don't have any wrongdoings. I didn't do anything."

"Don't be daft, boy. It doesn't matter whether you've done anything or not. It only matters that you're sorry and that you promise never to do it again."

"Never do again the thing I don't believe I did in the first place."

"Now you've got it."

"In the name of Cerberus, I read the name of a character from a T.S. Elliot poem! In a classroom! Even if some students find the name controversial or offensive, isn't the classroom where we should be discussing such matters, working them out?"

"Well, you'll have to sound a lot more contrite than that. Contrition is very important."

"I'm sorry," Socks said exasperated, "but I really don't understand what you're getting at."

"Much better," the Provost replied. "But keep the 'I'm sorry' and get rid of everything else, starting with how you 'really don't understand.' Come on, you talk and I'll type it up for you."

Hamhock squared up the keyboard in from of her. She could type, but only with some effort. When she first tried her hand (so to speak) it was easy to memorize the keyboard, but her trotters were so large and clumsy that typing something as simple as "Dear sir," came out "DCFSe4wrazxsreft5 sxdaijkrtgfd." Gradually she learned to hold a pencil between the two large toes of her trotters to more accurately type the correct letters, a method that shared some aspects of a gorilla threading a needle.

"D...e ...a...r," she typed for what seemed like minutes. "I a...m s...o...rr...y."

Socks nudged the pig out of the way, and she nearly lost her balance.

"I'll type," he said impatiently. "You can just look over my shoulder and make sure I say the right things."

"Oh, I don't know about that. An authentic apology really should come from you."

"Again, if I knew what I— oh, never mind." He set his paws on the keyboard, the front-most pads of his front paws poised above the D-F and J-K keys, with his dew claws poised above the space bar. This was the resting position for touch typing he had learned at a young age and even now he recalled the animal mnemonic he had practiced over and over again. "The quick red fox jumps over the lazy brown dog. The quick red fox jumps over the lazy brown dog." It had always annoyed him that the fox got the upper hand, but he could type out that sentence blindfolded—or perhaps it's better to say, with his eyes closed.

"Dear students, I am sorry."

"Brilliant," Hamhock said.

"Stop interrupting and let me do this," Socks said. He typed for about five-and-a-half minutes—the Provost might have taken an hour to type as many words—and, after a few revisions, this is what he came up with:

TO: the animal community at Aesop College
RE: the classroom incident

    I am so sorry that the discussion we had in class today offended anyone. I promise to make amends in any way I can, and I'll try to do better in the future.

    I am very, very sorry. Sincerely,
    —Socks

"Good enough?" the border collie asked the pig.

"Brilliant!" the Provost snorted. "Now hit the **PRINT** button and you're done. I have to rush to a meeting, but just give this to Mrs. Pilfer and she'll make copies and distribute them."

The Provost left her office with Socks still standing at the keyboard. The border collie reread his apology, his paw hovering over the **PRINT** button. He stared at the screen, looked out the window, then back at the screen. He began to type again.

> P.S.: I want to be honest with you, my fellow mammals, as well as any birds or reptiles that may have been affected. The classroom is a place where we can talk about any topic, even topics that you may not like. It's called academic freedom. That video from class that somebody posted, with its inflammatory, rabble-rousing headline, completely mischaracterizes what happened.
> I don't want to sound defensive, but it's way off base.
>> Even more sincerely,
>> Professor Socks, MACH, DEX, AEA

CHAPTER 3

As soon as the apology popped out of the printer, Socks gave it to Mrs. Pilfer, who made a few dozen copies and sent a student worker to post them around campus.

That was that, Socks thought. I've somehow offended the cats, but now I've apologized, and we can all move on.

Not so fast, said the collective animal consciousness. The rest of the animals hadn't had a chance to weigh in. By the following day the 500 views of the video had turned into 50,000. The animals on campus, even the squirrels, could talk of nothing else. The topic of the M-word and how a professor had said it in class became like the wildfire that threatened Bambi and all the other creatures of the forest.

Cats rarely left their dorms, but when they did, they traveled in clowders for fear they might encounter Socks and become unintended victims of his anti-cat-ite rhetoric. These clowders of cats did manage to make it to the Provost's office, where they lodged further complaints.

"We've been triggered," they said.

"We've been attacked."

"We've been injured."

In an unprecedented move, the Provost pulled Socks from the classroom, putting him in the doghouse in an extended "down-stay" until the matter could be sorted out.

"But I apologized," Socks argued.

"The cats refuse to accept your apology," the Provost replied. "They find it insincere. It could have something to do with your P.S."

"We've been triggered. We've been attacked."

Socks was silent.

Other canines on the faculty, nervous that they too might end up in trouble, barked and snarled at each other about whether the cats needed the faculty's protection. Most said yes. They argued about whether Socks was guilty of species-ism. This seemed to be about 50-50, but dogs were cautious about voicing an opinion. A red Bavarian fish hound named Jake, who taught English literature, defended Socks on the grounds of academic freedom, only to have all of the students and many of the faculty label him an anti-cat-ite. Defend an anti-cat-ite and you *are* an anti-cat-ite, so the thinking seemed to go. Another dog, a ragged grey mutt named Argos who taught zoology and anthropology, casually asserted that students had changed in the years since he began teaching, and how this sort of thing never used to happen, and how difficult it was to know what might be offensive and to whom.

Anti-cat-ite!

Many of the faculty wondered whether the Provost had done the right thing by removing a professor from teaching, but they were extra cautious in what they said out loud, and to whom. "Could this happen to me? Have I ever done anything in the classroom that would cause this response?" were the questions they pondered most often.

The rabbits had the brilliant idea of organizing a "we are listening" session, so that all the animals could come together and work through their issues. The Provost agreed and she called upon all the animals at the college to gather in the quad the next morning at sunrise for Aesop's first ever, all-campus, all-species "we are listening" session. She extended a special invitation to Socks, but strongly suggested that he "just listen."

No one got much sleep that night, least of all Socks. He arrived in the quad the next morning about twenty minutes before he expected the sun to rise and was surprised to find so many animals already present. He stood at the entrance to the quad and looked over the crowd.

All of the animals sat in a large circle. At first glance, Socks thought this might be a metaphor for the kind of egalitarian discussion the animals hoped to have. Witnessing the hyper vigilance of some of the non-predators, he realized their instinctive desire was to be able to see everyone else in the group all at once, in case any animal up the food chain got any ideas.

All of the cats sat on one side of the circle, next to the great elm. Robespierre and Magda, and Chiffon huddled together. Cleopatra struck a pose inspired by Egyptian hieroglyphs, but her attempt at queenliness was foiled by Tiny Tim, who nuzzled his head against her, then rolled on his back, batting his paws in the air and inviting her to play.

The dogs sat on the other side. Jake and Argos sat to one side of the pack. A greyhound named Guinefort eyed Nora the python, splayed across several branches of the elm on the other side of the quad. In spite of the desire to form a circle, an alpha Rottweiler named Buck, who taught sociology, sat in front of the other dogs and busily chewed an itchy spot on his rump. Other canine faculty members fell in behind Buck.

Otherwise, the rabbits huddled together in their group, joined by a few guinea pigs and a sugar glider. Lucifer the crow perched on the back of a park bench. Seated next to Lucifer was Jack Flash, a kangaroo (yes, a kangaroo!) who had recently joined Aesop's faculty to teach the pre-law courses. Flash, as he liked to be called, had been a comfort animal at Bigg State University, across the street, but he was evicted when Bigg State changed its policies toward comfort.

All around them, the squirrels continued doing their squirrely thing, oblivious to the import of the meeting that was about to happen. At least they stopped running in and out of the circle after several of the cats hissed at them.

As Socks entered the quad, Buck strode up to him and got in his grill. The Rottweiler had had a difficult life. As a puppy, he was put in a crate and thrown into the river to drown. He escaped, only to be adopted by thugs who ran dogfights. When the police broke up their ring, Buck was sent to a shelter and eventually became a rescue dog with a young, human college student who had also been abused in her childhood. Because of these experiences, Buck fancied himself a defender of the defenseless. Hence, even though he himself was not a cat and had no personal experience with the M–word, he nonetheless felt obliged to express outrage on the cats' behalf. Socks had heard from another dog that Buck was outraged by his actions in class, although, like many of the other dogs who held opinions on this subject, Buck had never bothered to ask Socks what had happened.

"This is a fireable offense!" the other dog reported Buck as saying. "A fireable offense!"

They stood muzzle to muzzle at the edge of the quad for several seconds, though it felt like hours. Buck was several paws taller than Socks. He looked down at him with anger in his eyes. He could easily deck me, Socks thought. This kind of macho, alpha-male fronting off was really not Socks's style, but in that moment, there was no way he was going to yield any ground. Other animals noticed the confrontation but took no action. The two dogs stood there like gladiatorial lions sizing each other up before pouncing. Socks spoke first.

"Do you want to ask me something?"

Buck did not respond. After a few more seconds of silence, Socks turned to walk away.

"Come back here," Buck said. "You asked me a question." Socks came back to where he stood and resumed his position, his muzzle just inches from Buck's. The Rottweiler raised his paw and pointed it at Socks.

"What you have to understand," Buck said in a measured but angry growl, "is that that word, for cats, is like an assault. It's like rape. It should never be said."

Socks held his intense glare, but he didn't hear any of Buck's words. He had become too angry himself.

"So, you don't want to ask me anything," Socks said, with just as much intensity.

Later, Socks would feel regret for that response. His question to Buck, "Do you want to ask me something?" was intended as an invitation. He wanted Buck to ask him what had happened in his class. He desperately wanted Buck not to have judged him before he had all the facts. It was Socks's way of saying, "You sniff my butt and I'll sniff yours and we'll recognize each other, and everything will be okay."

But Buck's anger didn't allow him to ask the question Socks wanted him to ask and he certainly was not going to sniff the border collie's butt. Buck responded out of his experience. Socks met anger with anger, the anger that comes from betrayal and abandonment.

"So, you don't want to ask me anything," Socks gnarled again. Two or three more seconds of them staring at each other and Socks left this encounter in disgust and found a place at the far end of the quad, in the circle, but not really associating with any of the animals there. If he'd bothered to look back, he might have seen the same disgust and disappointment on Buck's face. It was a classic example of two well-meaning and highly educated dogs who could not communicate with each other.

Finally, the Provost arrived. Hamhock took a seat among the rabbits, but in the back of the circle. This was not an event for displays of taxonomy. She was there to listen.

Professor Peeps, a grey, Velveteen Lop rabbit from the psychology department, hopped into the circle and opened the meeting.

"An incident has happened on our campus," Peeps began, "which has caused great suffering." He emphasized the first syllables of the words *in*cident and *suf*fering, to add emotional impact. "We are not here to judge," the rabbit continued, "but to attempt to practice restorative justice." Again, he repeated the phrase and added emphasis as before "To att*emp*t to *prac*tice re*stor*ative *jus*tice."

Argos leaned over and whispered to Jake.

"Peeps is perfect to lead this ... whatever *this* is," he said.

"And why?" Jake asked, already dreading the reason.

"All ears," Argos said and stifled a laugh.

"The most important thing for restorative justice," Peeps said, "is relationship. Every relationship is important. In fact, our relationships are more important than how anyone might feel in the moment." Peeps drew attention to the fact that all the animals were sitting in a circle.

"We need communication, listening, and apology," he continued. "Sitting in this circle, as community, we need to make decisions as a community, which includes everyone in the community." All of this sounded promising. His tone was calm and measured and coming from a rabbit, addressing such a large crowd, his words were even more compelling.

"We stand as *all*ies with our students," he concluded. "We want to *lis*ten to you, to help *amp*lify your voices and to hear what *you* need. But sitting in the *cir*cle, we *must* remember that the *most* important task is to re*store* our re*lation*ships."

The next few minutes were like that moment when a predator is stalking its prey, both animals frozen in silence, each waiting for the other to make the first move. A circle discussion had no authority at its head calling on speakers, so everyone had to wait for someone to be moved. When students finally got the chance to weigh in, it did not seem that their voices needed amplifying.

"The use of the M-word excludes cats," Robespierre firmly stated. "Professor Jake's defense of Professor Socks on the grounds of academic freedom was disappointing. This wasn't academic freedom, which is just a thing that privilege-ed dogs hide behind! We need immediate redress, including a re-evaluation of the curriculum!"

Chiffon stood to "echo and amplify" Robespierre's comments.

"Humans send their cats here to be safe!" she said. "This is a breach of trust and safety! This is not about tenure, and the idea that you can say something that hurtful and be sheltered by the institution is not right! It's a form of species-ism! If your body's not affected by that word, you don't get to use it! If students have to beg you to keep them safe, why—" She paused, clearly affected by her emotions. "This is not about academic freedom! History and context matters. Are we committed to this work or not? We need to place an order of protection around this idea."

It went on like this for a while. Students, mostly the cats, but a few of the guinea pigs, yowled and yammered for something like an hour. Provost Hamhock sat silently, keeping her eyes on the canine faculty, who followed her lead. At the end of the "we are listening" session, another rabbit, a French Angora named Babette, who had helped to organize the event, called on the faculty to support the students.

"Some-zing 'aas to 'appen," Babette said, in what sounded like a Parisian accent, though it could have been from Languedoc. "We are try-éeng to do zis. Eet won't be zee laast 'we are leestening' sessión."

"We want action!" a cat in the circle shouted. "We're tired of just words. Something has to be done!"

This last cry was followed by awkward silence. Slowly, the crowd dispersed and the "we are listening" session was over.

Socks was still sitting at the far end of the quad. He just sat there, waiting to see if anyone would approach him, either in anger or in solidarity. A Chihuahua named Toni, who taught chemistry, walked over and sniffed his butt, then looked up at the border collie and wagged her tiny tail.

"You're brave," Socks whispered in Toni the Chihuahua's ear. She shrugged her shoulders and smiled.

Guinefort the greyhound, an adjunct in philosophy who specialized in the writings of the human Saint Augustine, told Socks that he needed to apologize and "sound contrite." He thought he was contrite about hurting the students' feelings, but this was not the contrition that she meant. He would need to be sorry for using the M-word. But he wasn't. This was part of a class discussion ... Oh, fuck it, he thought to himself.

There was another listening session the next day. This one was held in the park adjacent to the campus, in hopes that a larger venue might bring out more students. It did. The huge crowd tried to sit in a single circle, but the circle's diameter was so large that the animals had to yell across it to be heard.

Acoustics were so bad that some animals started moving inside the circle just to understand what their fellow animals were saying. For a while, they formed several concentric circles, but these soon collapsed, and the shape of the group became more amorphous, more of an amoeba than a geometric symbol of egalitarianism. Perhaps as a result of this, students at the meeting showed little to no concern for restorative justice.

Things heated up. There was talk about rejecting the idea of academic freedom, about getting rid of tenure, about the administration not circling the wagons to protect anti-cat-ite professors. Some of the non-feline animals tried to show solidarity with the cats.

"I'm so sorry this happened," said a reddish guinea pig with white spots. "I want to be your ally. I want to help, but I don't know what I should do."

"If you don't know what you should do then you're a species-ist!" said Robespierre.

Argos tried to offer his understanding of the events on campus, and what he thought canine allies might do.

"Stop your 'dog-splaining,'" Chiffon interrupted. "You old-dog-who-can't-learn-new-tricks anti-cat-ite!"

Tiny Tim suddenly stood up and froze in place. His face seemed red with anger. He opened his mouth wide, revealing his fangs, but no words came out. He had a look of suppressed rage, of ire that had been held in for so long that it made him gag. He began retching. The contractions and convulsions in his stomach muscles were visible. Gag, retch, cough, gag, cough. The animals around him made room for whatever fury-filled rant was about to come. One final cough and ...

Ack. Aaack!

"Hairball," said Tiny Tim with an embarrassed laugh.

The second listening session was not as successful as the first, at least if one judges by the amount of listening that was not done. Socks again received sympathetic words from several colleagues, though after the Jake and Argos debacles, few of them were willing to risk speaking up in public, either in support of Socks or in favor of academic freedom. Some of his colleagues' comments offered a kind of passive-aggressive, conditional support. For example, Guinefort sent a note with the subject line, "Peace be with you."

"I've been wanting to write but not sure what to say," she wrote. "I don't agree with your moves in the classroom, but that is not what this email is about ..." There followed some very nice sentiment that could have come right out of the handbook of pastoral care. But why start with "I don't agree with your moves"? Socks wondered. You don't know what my moves were, he thought. You didn't ask me!

"Well, I may not agree with what you did," wrote one of the bitches who was not on the faculty, "but I'm wondering how you're doing." Screw you, Socks thought. How is it possible to agree or disagree with what I did, he wondered, without knowing all the facts? The female dog closed her note, "This all feels fraught and reactive, on all sides." Yes, Socks thought. And that fraught-ness and reactivity is coming from you!

The prevailing attitude, the mood on campus, was that supporting and protecting the students was the most important thing. The final straw was a petition put out by Buck and two Jack Russell terriers, one named Cindy and the other named Cyndi, who felt especially protective of their feline students. It read as follows:

> We, the undersigned faculty of Aesop College, find Professor Socks's use of the M-word harmful, hurtful, hateful, and harassing. Dogs have always used this word to humiliate cats and rob them of their essential animalism. Things only got worse when Socks defended his use of the M-word in the guise of an apology, which was anything but.
>
> Professor Jake argued that this is a matter of academic freedom. Deer ticks and ring worms! We reject, renounce, repudiate, and refute this claim! Academic freedom is no excuse for hurting students' feelings and such claims only fuel institutional species-ism. Our faculty, mostly the dogs (especially the dogs), must be more self-critical in their positions of power, and more woke to their species identity and privilege. We say this as dogs ourselves.
>
> Academic freedom for animals means freedom from species-ism, from rampant anti-cat-ite harassment and

> discrimination, and from oppression and trauma at the hands of faculty (mostly the dogs). We faculty (especially the dogs) must be humble before our students, in order to protect their feelings, and respect their highest animal nature.

There followed several suggestions on how the college might combat species-ism, ideas that even Socks found to be quite reasonable. The petition was signed by half the faculty, but there was the catch. If some animal signed just because they liked the good suggestions at the end of the petition, they were by default also endorsing the idea that Socks and the others were anti-cat-ites. It was impossible to agree to one without agreeing to the other. Socks and Jake were in the library when the petition was published. They read it silently together.

"All I did was read a word out loud, just as the author had written it!" Socks tried but failed to whisper. "A fucking WORD! Owooooo!"

"Shhh!" Jake said, reminding his friend where they were. "You're not handling this well." Master of understatement, Socks thought, as he quietly stewed and held his colleagues in contempt.

After two days of "we are listening" sessions, President Sourgrapes, the fox, sent out a note with actions the college planned to take, including a full investigation of the events in Socks's classroom and further allegations that students had raised against him. His note ended as follows:

> Safety is our number one priority, ~~deer~~ dear students. But you have to take risks in college, otherwise your ~~little~~ cat brains won't grow. But not too many risks, otherwise your ~~little~~ cat brains won't grow.
>
> Growing your brains is what college is all about. But it must be done safely. We ~~shouldn't~~ ~~won't~~ can't confuse

intellectual safety with emotional safety. Or physical safety. The one is about your brain, while the others are about your heart and your body. But ~~the key to safety is in your *paws*~~ the key to safety is in *your* paws. Remember the motto of the wise old ~~fox~~ owl, who once said, "No safety, know pain." How true. How true.

The next time you look in the mirror, say to yourself, "You are looking at the animal responsible for your safety." So, stay alert and don't get hurt. Speak up if your feelings ever get scared and ~~my administration~~ I will do everything I can to lessen your scared-ness.

Without you, ~~delicious~~ dear students, Aesop College would not exist. Each one of you is ~~a specialty~~ special. We believe you have just as much to teach us as we have to teach you. And for any students I've not yet met, I look forward to ~~eating~~ meeting you.

CHAPTER 4

The faculty lounge was busy that afternoon.

They called it the faculty lounge, but of course it was just the old dog park on the edge of campus. The gate had broken long ago, so any animal could come and go as they pleased.

There was no grass in the park on account of all the running and stick chasing the dogs had done there over the decades, but a shady catalpa tree graced the center of the park. In spite of all the noise the dogs made, you could still hear birds chirping as they hid amidst the catalpa's large leaves. Draped over one of the catalpa branches, a crusty, one-eyed cat named Obadiah lay in wait for his dinner. No longer outfitted with a parallax view, the aging predator now had to wait for the birds to come to him.

There was nary a human in sight. Other than Obadiah, it was just dogs. Socks, Jake, and Argos lay in the dusty patch that surrounded the catalpa. Toni the Chihuahua was there. Cindy and Cyndi, the two Jack Russell terriers, chased each other around the perimeter of the fence, avoiding eye contact with the larger dogs at the center. There were also five pups of questionable lineage, though most suspected that Argos was somehow involved. The pups (three dogs and two bitches) had recently been whelped and had taken the names of the five Marx brothers: Groucho, Chico, and Harpo for the males. Zeppo and Gummo for the females. The five of them stumbled and wrestled over each other with great vigor, to the amusement of their elders. Buck and Guinefort were nowhere to be seen.

Other than Obadiah, it was just dogs.

Socks let out a long sigh and plopped his head down on his crossed forelegs. Argos began to pant nervously. Jake kept an eye on the speed-crazy Russells.

"Can you believe Sourgrapes's note?" Socks said at last.

"The president's an idiot," Jake said, then quickly looked around.

"Never underestimate a fox," Socks said. "There's always more going on than you can see on the surface. But still ..."

Jake and Argos both nodded. Socks continued.

"I agree with Sourgrapes that intellectual safety is antithetical to learning. One must take intellectual risks to learn. But I challenge the idea that emotional safety is required—that without emotional safety, students will be unable to learn. Has this animal never listened to a piece of music or experienced a painting in a museum? Has he never attended a play? We must make ourselves unsafe in order to learn anything from a work of art."

Jake and Argos, now joined by Toni the Chihuahua, made sing-song vocalizations to express their agreement. Socks went on.

"When we watch *Oedipus Rex*, it's *possible* to sit there and *intellectually* conclude that killing one's sire and sleeping with one's dam is not good. But the ancient Greeks understood that, to really "get it," one had to give up emotional safety, to become *vulnerable*, to experience *catharsis*. How dare Sourgrapes promise the students that they would be *emotionally* safe? If that ever happened, their educations would be robbed of essential animal experience."

"Brrr-urrr-oo-iirr-ooo," the other dogs whimpered with furrowed brows. Socks was on a roll now.

"Another thing. Sourgrapes's note conflates emotional safety with physical safety. Buck came up to me as I arrived at the 'listening session,' stuck his slobber-drenched muzzle right in my face and said, 'For cats, that word is an assault. It's like rape.'"

The three dogs listening to Socks registered shock. This was the first they'd heard of the encounter with Buck.

"I don't presume to understand the feelings of other animals, nor do I wish to rob them of any emotions they choose to feel. But I do think it's reasonable to insist on some precision of language.

"It's interesting that Buck's rant used two figures of speech: a metaphor ('the word *is* an assault') and a simile ('it's *like* rape'). The simile seems apt. Words can evoke feelings so strong that they cause the listener to recall violent events. But the metaphor becomes less powerful, even ridiculous, when people start believing that it is not a metaphor, but reality.

"Can a word actually *be* an assault? There are verbal assaults, of course, but I think that's also intended metaphorically. It's not *the same as a physical assault*. Again, I don't want to deny the feelings cats have. But if a word is literally an assault, does that mean that the police and the court system and the dog catcher should get involved to mete out justice and punishment?"

No one noticed that the two Russells had stopped racing and slowly moved closer to hear what Socks was saying. Socks was a forceful lecturer who never used notes, spoke seemingly impromptu, and always wowed his students. Some would even say "*bow*-wowed." When he had finished, all the dogs in the park were looking at him. Socks had not been in the classroom all week and he realized he was missing that rush.

Suddenly, one of the pups, Zeppo, no, Gummo (it was still hard to tell) jumped full force onto Socks's back and laughed as he tumbled to the ground.

"What's Mungojerrie?" Gummo asked as he looked up at the border collie.

"You really shouldn't say that word," Jake offered.

"Why?" Gummo asked.
"It's just not a word we should say."
"Why?"
"It's a name ... a term ... the cats don't like," said Socks.
"Why?" Gummo insisted.
"Why? Why? Why?" the three Marx brothers and one Marx sister chimed in.

Socks took a deep breath and assumed his teacherly voice.

"Mungojerrie is the name of a cat, a character in a poem by a human named T.S. Elliot. Mungojerrie's partner in the poem is another cat named Rumpleteazer. Mungojerrie and Rumpleteazer," he paused. It felt good just to say the names as part of a discussion and not have to look over his shoulder.

"Elliot, the human poet, describes Mungojerrie and Rumpleteazer as thieves. And while they seem charming in the poem, to be called a thief is actually a terrible insult, and this is why the cats don't like it."

"Is that what you think?" Jake barked in disbelief. "That's not at all the problem with that word."

"Oh? Enlighten me ... us."

"Mungo is a classic boy's name in Scotland. There was a St. Mungo, whose real name was Kentigern, the patron saint of Glasgow.

"Mungo's mother was a human princess named Thaney, the daughter of a Scottish king who ruled in the 6th century. She became pregnant by Yvain, whom you know from the stories of Arthur and his knights of the Round Table. There are different versions of whether Yvain and Thaney were in love, or whether he raped her. In any case, her father, the king, was enraged that she was pregnant and threw her off the high walls of Traprain Law, a fortress atop a high Scottish ben, or mountain. She survived long enough to give birth, but her dead and broken body was eaten by feral cats, who also licked the newborn baby clean before dragging him to a cave in the mountain side.

"A hermit named Serf found the baby and chased off all the cats. He adopted the boy and gave him the name Mungo, which in the old language meant 'little pet,' because that's what he seemed to be to the wild cats. Mungo knew nothing of his royal lineage, of his beautiful mother or cruel grandfather. How could he? The only origin story he knew was that the wild cats had killed his mother, 'ripping him from her womb,' as Serf told it, and carrying him off to their lair for God knows what purpose."

The pups sat in rapt attention as Jake continued.

"The medieval *Life of Mungo*, written some centuries later, tells of three miracles that the saint performed, all of them connected to the evildoing of cats. He saved a bird that had been attacked by cats and caused it to fly again. He repaired and saved a tree that cats had pissed on and used as a scratching post to the point of destruction. The tree lived for many more years and bore fruit that fed all the peasants in the valley."

"Oooh," said the wide-eyed pups.

"I suppose we might more rightly call the final miracle an 'almost miracle.' A human king suspected his queen of infidelity and accused her of leaving her wedding ring with her lover. He demanded to see the ring, but she couldn't find it. In reality, the king himself had thrown the ring into the River Clyde. Facing execution, the queen called on Mungo the holy man for help. Mungo ordered his servant to catch a fish in the river and bring it back to the castle. This would count among the greatest magic tricks of all time: the ring was inside the fish."

The puppies gasped in amazement.

"All Mungo needed to do was carve the fish open to expose the ring and the queen would be saved."

At this point, all the pups, as well as the adult dogs leaned in. Even Cyndi and Cindy gave all their attention to the story, without displaying an ounce of nervous energy. Jake paused even longer, making eye contact with each one of the dogs. They marveled at Jake's skills as a storyteller. He continued.

"But ... *a goddamned feral cat* leapt onto the table and *stole* the fish! The miracle was ruined, and the queen was beheaded the next morning!

"What?" the puppy named Groucho yapped.

"From that day forward, Mungo dedicated his life to driving the cats out of Scotland, much as St. Patrick drove the snakes out of Ireland." Jake finished his story and the canine audience nearly collapsed from exhaustion. They sat in silence until one of the Marx sisters (Gummo, no Zeppo) let loose a long whine.

"Nooooooo!"

Socks thought for a bit longer before responding.

"So, cats hate the term Mungo," Socks said, "because they see this medieval holy man as a great cat killer. In fact, as a perpetrator of mass felinocide."

"I'm afraid so," Jake confirmed.

From his perch on the catalpa branch, Obadiah the cat rolled his single eye.

"No, no, no," Argos said with a hint of disdain. "That's not why the cats hate the M-word."

This was something new, the young pups thought. Was this what was meant by scholarly disagreement? Would there be a fight? They looked for Jake to bare his teeth but saw no signs of aggression.

"Let me tell you the real story," Argos said.

As if choreographed, all the dogs stood up, circled the ground beneath their feet several times, then resettled, with their bodies re-focused away from Jake and in the direction of Argos. They had heard from the lit prof, now they would hear from the anthropologist.

"Long ago, in ancient Egypt, during the reign of the human pharaohs, cats were revered as gods. This was also the time when the Egyptians enslaved the Jews, the time of

Moses and the Exodus and the parting of the Red Sea. A time when humans put their faith in the god YHWH.

"After their Exodus, their 'exit' from Egypt, some of the Jews turned away from YHWH and began worshipping a cow. As animals," Argos paused for effect. "As animals, we naturally find cow worship very reasonable. Even logical. A cow is real. It gives you milk and can keep you warm on a frosty winter night. YHWH, on the other hand, was unseen and his gifts, if you could call them that, were often unpredictable. In spite of the extremely reasonable practice of worshipping cows, the human Moses tried to stop it. Some of the Jews accepted this and returned to YHWH. Others split off from the group and began to wander across the land."

"What about the cats?" Harpo asked.

"Yes, the cats, the cats," the other pups yapped.

"We're getting to that," Argos said. "Some of these wandering Jews who split off from the main group travelled from Egypt toward the setting sun. Their leader was a man named Melek, who had actually been a guard in Pharaoh's palace. Melek had seen how the Egyptians had worshipped cats. 'If cats could give power to the pharaoh,' he thought, 'maybe we should take a few cats and worship them, too.' Melek led his tribe from Egypt, south along the Nile, across the land which the humans now call Nigeria, but which the ancestors knew as *egerew n-igerewen*. Eventually, Melek and his people and the cats arrived at a place called Cameroon."

"What does this have to do with Mungojerrie?" Toni the Chihuahua asked, her body frenetic.

"I'm getting to that," Argos barked.

"This small tribe of cat-worshipping Jews wandered and wandered, all over Africa. They got lost many times, until they finally settled in the place called Cameroon. They settled in the Mungo valley, on the banks of the Mungo River. Soon the neighboring tribes came to call Melek and his people the Mungo."

"Aahh," the pups collectively sighed. Now things were making sense.

"Remember, Melek had brought two cats on the journey. But where there are two cats there are soon many cats. Melek intended to worship the cats hoping they would bring prosperity to his people, but he really had no idea how to do this. He knew the Egyptians worshipped cats, but he knew none of their rituals.

"So, the cats were ignored and then began to multiply, and multiply some more and soon they became a nuisance to the Mungo humans. They would steal the Mungo's food and tip over Mungo milk barrels so they could lap up the milk. Seeking warmth during a strangely cold winter, many of the cats sneaked into the Mungo babies' cribs and (unintentionally) suffocated them. The Mungo mothers went on a rampage and carried out a great cat massacre—rivaled only by the Great Cat Massacre of Paris, in 1730. Thousands of cats were killed, their bodies mutilated and thrown into the Mungo River. It was one of the worst moments in feline history."

"And ever since then cats have hated the word Mungo?" Zeppo said.

"Spot on," Argos said and nuzzled the puppy with his snout.

"What about Jerrie?" Gummo asked. "It's Mungo*jerrie*. What about the *Jerrie*?"

"Excellent question," said Argos. "You are all brilliant pups indeed." Gummo jumped on him and wanted to wrestle, so happy was she to get his approval.

"Okay. The 'jerrie' in Mungojerrie comes much later, during a time that the humans call the nineteenth century. Cameroon had become a colony of the German Empire. The Germans exploited the labor and other resources of the Mungo, who were still around, even though they no longer possessed any cats. There were still cats in the Mungo Valley.

The survivors of the Massacre at Mungo, as it came to be known, had repopulated the area, though all the cats were feral.

"Anyway, the Germans moved in as colonizers and a rather obnoxious epithet for them was 'Jerrie.' In the Mungo Valley, they were called 'Mungojerries.' In truth, the Mungojerries were fairly decent toward the feral cats they encountered, but over time their name was conflated with the ancient Mungo, who had massacred all the cats."

"And ever since then cats have hated the word Mungo*jerrie*!" Zeppo exclaimed.

Spot on," Argos said. "Spot on."

The dogs stood and stretched and tamped down the earth with their pads to resettle. Over their heads, Obadiah had no response except to shake his head.

"But you know," Toni the Chihuahua said with an impish smile. "That's not the real reason cats hate the word Mungojerrie."

Barking and howling and even some snarling. All five puppies proceeded to chase each other in a ring around the group. It was getting to be too much. How many origin stories could Mungojerrie have? Toni the Chihuahua smiled at the rise her comment had gotten.

"If you want to know the real story, you have to know a human song from the 1970s called 'In the summertime.'"

"Ah, Mungojerry," Socks said with a smile, then turned to the pups to explain. "That was the name of a band."

"One of the greatest, one-hit wonders of the 70s," said Argos. "And the sideburns on that guy! He must have a place in the human facial hair hall of fame!"

"Great song!" Jake added. "Carefree and light-hearted. It could almost have been written by a dog."

"It *was* written by a dog," Toni the Chihuahua said, but from her tone it was clear she meant 'dawg,' as in 'player,' or 'ladies' man.'

"What do you mean?" Socks asked.

"Well, it's totally sexist," she said. "And classist."

"Huh?"

"Oh, come on, daaawg. If her sire's *rich* take her out for a meal. If her sire's *poor*, just *do what you feel*! That's a horrible way to think about bitches."

"Do you mean bitches? Or *bitches*?"

Toni the Chihuahua just stared at him. She tried not to break, but a snippet of laughter escaped through her wet nose.

"You—" Socks realized he'd been had. Then they both laughed out loud and rolled in the dirt, as the other dogs watched them.

"And ever since then," Zeppo said, "cats have hated the word Mungojerrie."

No longer able to withhold comment, and safely out of the dogs' reach, Obadiah yelled down from the catalpa tree.

"You dumb-ass, bohunk fleabags don't know scat about cats," he said. "Someday, somebody's gonna pay for all this witlessness!"

Like a pack of synchronized swimmers, all the dogs looked up in a single, graceful gesture and registered the cat lingering above them. Then, just as quickly, they returned to their own business. Socks gave Zeppo a look and a nudge—the invitation to play—and Zeppo took off, knowing Socks would chase her. He pursued the pup all around the park, followed by the rest of the pack, all gleefully laughing and yapping and running and chasing, just for the joy of it.

Except for Cyndi and Cindy, who had slinked off to find Buck.

CHAPTER 5

While the dogs were cavorting in the faculty lounge, telling origin stories about the M-word, the cats had called a special meeting of the Feline Activist Student Council: Safety Team, or FASC:ST. They felt that action had to be taken against Professor Socks.

Robespierre and Chiffon were conducting the meeting from a classroom in Old Main. Magda, Cleopatra, and Tiny Tim were all in attendance, as were about six or seven other cats. Not all of them had been in the class where the incident happened, but they were there to express cat solidarity.

Over 150 other cats among Aesop's student body did not attend the meeting, choosing instead to do their homework or nap in a sunny spot on a library shelf. Several groups of cats throughout the dorms sat in circles taking hits of catnip from a thimble before passing it around, on their way to catatonic bliss. Now and again, a Boston terrier named Kojak strolled down the hall, acting as a kind of dorm monitor. Kojak was not the brightest Beta in the pack and he never realized that the tap-tap-tapping of his overgrown toenails always gave away his position.

"Cheese it! The cops!" One of the loopy cats would say when they heard him coming, as they stashed their stash behind a litter box and dissolved in laughter.

Also present at the FASC:ST meeting were a few non-felines, animals who called themselves "allies." These included Nora the python, as well as Professor Babette and Professor Peeps, the two rabbits who had led the "we are list-

The cats had called a special meeting.

ening" sessions. Professor Buck was the FASC:ST faculty adviser, so he was there, and Professor Guinefort was there, well, because Buck was there.

"It's outrageous," Robespierre said, opening the meeting, "that in this day and age a professor at this college would say the M-word, out loud, in a class full of cats!"

General caterwauling. Yes! How dare he? The nerve!

"That's not the only time he's done it," Chiffon said. "I heard he says it all the time, especially when no one's around and he thinks we can't hear him."

"I heard him myself, one day when I was sitting on the highest branches of the quad elm and he was walking below," Tiny Tim said.

"I hear that even when he's not saying it, he's thinking it," Magda added in disgust.

"Something has to be done," Robespierre said.

"Yes!" the cat collective collectively said. "Something ... Something has to be done!" Some of them grumbled and yowled. Some of them paced back and forth as if they were tigers in cages while others jumped up on desks and hissed, tails flicking, at imaginary beings.

Buck cleared his throat and raised a paw.

"The FASC:ST recognizes Professor Buck," said Robespierre.

"First," Buck said, "I want to acknowledge the power differential in the room. I'm a professor and you are all students. You are cats and I'm a dog, and I can only speak from my point of view." The cats purred their approval. Buck continued.

"This is clearly a serious matter. Very serious. In all the years that I've been teaching here, I can't recall an incident like this, that has caused so much pain and emotional hurt, that has literally turned the campus upside down."

If Socks had been there, he would have taken issue with Buck's use of "literally" when what he really meant was "figuratively" or "metaphorically."

No matter. Behind his bloodshot brown eyes, Buck imagined the figure of Socks standing in front of him. Smug, Buck thought. Arrogant, too. Always acting like he's the pick of the litter.

"Robespierre is right. Something must be done. But I urge you to consider your options and choose the most effective tactics."

"I'd like to scratch his eyes out!" Magda yowled.

"Yes. I'm sure that might feel good," Buck said. "But will it affect the change you want? Think about how the great social movements worked. From Gandhi's non-violence to the protests during United States v. Fritz the Cat, whether you choose passive resistance or direct action, armed rebellion or artistic agitprop, you must have a plan. As Tigger X used to say, 'You can't stick it to the man, if you don't have a plan. After that, you can bite 'em on the can and shake 'em till the chicken's in the pan.'"

Chiffon and Magda rushed up to Buck and started weaving between his legs, rubbing against him and head-butting his chest. Tiny Tim rolled on his back and batted his paws in the air, his body wiggling, his tail swishing. Robespierre sat back, nodding to Buck in approval.

Guinefort, in a statuesque "sit," raised an elegant paw.

"The FASC:ST recognizes Professor Guinefort," said Robespierre.

"What resources do you ... I mean, I'm an adjunct, and a dog, and I speak from my privilege. Okay? So, what resources do you have at your disposal? What information or evidence can you bring?"

The cats pondered for a while and then Cleopatra said, "The video."

"The video!" the other cats repeated.

Guinefort went to the classroom's computer terminal and called up the video on ZooTube. The number of views now counted over a million. The cats looked at each other with glee as they saw this. Guinefort hit play.

"Mungojerrie and Rumpleteazer ..." Socks said at the very start of the video.

"There it is," Robespierre said. "That's a heart-piercing indictment right there."

"Yes," Guinefort said. "But it isn't enough on its own. You need to show the pain and suffering he caused."

Just as she said this, they could hear the cats off camera crying out, and then see their reactions: flattened ears, blinking eyes, exposed fangs. Robespierre looked toward Guinefort, gestured to the computer screen and shrugged his shoulders, as if to say, "Well, there you have it."

Then the Socks in the video said, "I need to ask you a difficult and dangerous question."

"A question!" Magda yowled. "Why does he have to ask us a question? Doesn't he know that questions violate my personal space? Doesn't he know questions can trigger us?"

Nora the python, seeing how upset Magda was, slowly and gently coiled herself around her fluffy-furred body. The Persian cat kneaded the snake's scales with her pads, as if preparing a bed.

"Look how he's looking at us," Cleopatra said. "He's making direct eye contact with every single cat in the room."

"It freaked me out," said Tiny Tim.

"He's just trying to connect," said Professor Peeps. "Canine communication is much diff—."

"Please raise your paw if you want to add to the discourse," Robespierre said to Peeps. "The FASC:ST did not recognize you. And before you speak, be sure to acknowledge your privilege."

"I'm just a rabbit," said Peeps.

"Too late," Robespierre said. "Move on."

They turned their attention back to the video.

"Quoting from an author's work," said video Socks, "was it appropriate to say the word 'Mungojerrie'?"

"There." Chiffon leapt in. "He said it again. He's said it twice now. I remember how I could feel Robespierre's entire body stiffen up when he said it the second time."

"And what's all this 'quoting from an author's work' nonsense?" It was Cleopatra again, who had now moved to a desktop where she sat like the Great Sphynx of Giza. "I think he's just using that as a way to give himself permission to say the word. He wants to titillate; be the 'dangerous, risk-taking professor.'"

The cats collectively purred their approval.

"Wasn't substituting the euphemistic phrase 'the M-word' for Mungojerrie, in fact, a disservice to T.S. Elliot's great poetry?"

Chiffon hit the pause button. She couldn't take it anymore. It was the straw that broke the camel's back—although Chiffon certainly would not have used that expression to describe her distress, not wishing to disparage the differently abled, or camels, even though she had never met one. She then launched into a diatribe against T.S. Elliot and why Socks had even chosen that poet in the first place.

"Did you know that Elliot was an anti-Semite?" she raged.

"What's a Semite?" Tiny Tim asked.

"It's a kind of human religion," Robespierre said.

"It's the humans who practice that religion,' Cleopatra said from on high, perhaps tapping into some historic memory still lodged in her DNA. "Think of the Semites as a species, one that many humans have oppressed throughout the centuries."

"Species-ism," said Tiny Tim.

"Precisely," said Cleopatra.

Professor Babette raised her petite paw.

"The FASC:ST recognizes Professor Babette."

"Yes. *Merci. Je suis* Babette. I am Babette. I am a *lapine*, a rabbéet and a *professeur* ... uhh, *bien sûr*, I only speak from my *point de vue, mais*, I must agree zat Elliot was a real anti-*Sémite*." She then pursued a tangent on the scholarly tradition that tracked anti-Semitism in Elliot's work. Bloom. Steiner. Fenton. All of them found traces of Jew-hating in Elliot's poems: stuff about rats underneath piles of something and Jews under the rats and money and furs. What could be more obvious?

Peeps considered pointing out that the rats might take issue with this as well, always being metaphorically linked to filth and evil and the most despicable aspects of life, even though rats were quite sociable and extremely intelligent. But just as he considered how he might preface his thoughts with a positional preamble—"I'm a rabbit and a professor ... no, professor and rabbit"—he was cut off.

"I think this is getting way off topic." It was Buck, who had spoken without being recognized, causing Professor Peeps to glare up at him. Robespierre also gave Buck a look and the Rottweiler was silenced.

"I agree with Professor Buck," Robespierre said. "What do we care about the humans and their belief systems and their anti-whatever-ism? We are animals, and, with all due respect for the struggles of other species, we should focus on animal concerns."

Members of the FASC:ST and their allies continued to dissect and deconstruct the video. They pointed out how Socks continued to use the M-word throughout the video, in spite of the students' protests. They raged at how he mocked them when he substituted euphemisms for the epithets.

"M-word and R-word were a very notorious couple of cats."

He said this in a whiny sing-song voice, like a baby saying "nanny-nanny-boo-boo." Disgusting.

Just as they finished watching the video, Cyndi and Cindy, the two Jack Russells, burst into the room to report the goings-on in the faculty lounge.

"And then ..." Cyndi said.

"And then ..." Cindy said.

Cats ran around the room in a frenzy, bounced off the walls, and unraveled window shades.

"Felines," Robespierre said. "Felines. Come to order. We have to make a plan."

"I still want to scratch his eyes out," Magda said again. Her back was arched and her claws dug into Nora's coils, but the python did not respond.

"No," Robespierre said. "No. I acknowledge your feelings and they are valid. This is a safe space and I admire you for being so upfront in sharing. But we need a plan that will have a bigger impact. Does anyone have a motion?"

Chiffon raised her paw.

"Uh, Chiffon. Cat. Student. This is just my opinion, but I think we should take the media campaign beyond ZooTube. Really make it go feral."

"Go feral! Go feral!" the cats all cheered, and they rubbed their bodies against one another and began chattering about all the ways they might spread their message. Professor Socks was going down and going down hard.

Buck and Guinefort looked at each other as if to say, "mission accomplished," then left the room.

Meanwhile, across campus, Reynaldo Sourgrapes had called an emergency meeting of the President's Univocal Council. The PUnC, as it was called, was a small task force made up of President Sourgrapes, Provost Hamhock, Mrs. Pilfer (whose job it was to take notes and implement decisions), and one other member, the special assistant to the president, who had not yet arrived. Sourgrapes had created the PUnC to address the discord sweeping Aesop's campus, to keep the messaging consistent, and, most importantly, to keep any of the cats and other students from dropping out for reasons of distress or emotional trauma.

"Our students are very fragile," President Sourgrapes said.

"We've already lost three little kittens," said Mrs. Pilfer, looking over a spreadsheet.

Upon hearing this news, Sourgrapes looked at the floor and shook his head. Hamhock asked where the kittens had gone and if anyone knew why they had dropped out.

"Unclear," said Mrs. Pilfer. "But it seems to be connected to a loss of mittens, at least that's the initial report."

"This is a very disturbing trend," said President Sourgrapes. "We simply cannot any longer afford to have kittens losing their mittens. We must reduce this practice that so clearly leads to a downward enrollment trend. Very disturbing!"

"Very disturbing," Provost Hamhock repeated, cowering as the president continued.

"We've done such a good job of diversifying the campus," Sourgrapes said. "What started as a movement to gain equality for comfort animals has now grown into something much bigger. All sorts of humans are sending their pets to Aesop College. But we're not the only one."

Indeed, many other colleges and universities across the country had adopted Aesop's practice of offering animals the opportunity of higher education. The trend was so successful that the prestigious ivy league schools considered rebranding themselves as "animal league" schools. But mammals running campuses and teaching other mammals was not without its rough spots. At Yowl University, on the east coast, cats in one of the dormitories attacked the service dogs who were there to protect them when they perceived the dogs as anti-cat-ite. With fangs bared and claws out, they drove the service dogs from their campus. When Middlepurry College in Vermont invited two human speakers—one from the American Kennel Club and one from the Cat Fanciers' Association—cats and dogs alike chased them from the stage and all the way to the edge of town, nipping at their heels, for advocating conformity to breed standards. Even Barkley University in California, which claimed to be the birthplace of animals in higher ed, had seen scandal rock their school when a pure-bred, provocative German shepherd came to speak on their campus. Every animal with four legs—dogs, cats, pigs, rats, sugar gliders, guinea pigs, even the squirrels—joined in protests, barking and hissing and growling and chirruping so loudly that the speaker couldn't be heard.

The spoken word wasn't the only thing that cats might find offensive. Images could also set them off. At Hamster University in the Midwest, an Airedale art history prof dared to show her students the depiction of an Egyptian cat-goddess in Duchamp's Cubist masterpiece, "Bastet Descending a Staircase." Some cats protested the painting as idolatry, even though the ancient Egyptians themselves had rendered their goddess in stone. Hamster's administration accused the professor of felino-phobia!

All these incidents eventually appeared on ZooTube and other local and national mediums. This was the atmosphere of all the schools that allowed comfort animals to teach and learn on their campuses. The pundits of higher education called it "bark out" culture, a curious phenomenon that made a campus unwelcome to any creature that did not adhere to the received animal orthodoxy. Any campus that became known for promoting species-ism risked losing its students, which was especially difficult for smaller schools like Aesop.

Mrs. Pilfer took furious notes, not in the sense that she took them furiously (in great haste), but because her notes contained all the fury that Sourgrapes was now unleashing on his leadership team. The fox paced back and forth so quickly that his lithe body became a tight S-shaped blur as his bushy tail seemed to crack like a whip with every turn.

"To top things off," Sourgrapes said, "we've been put on notice from the ASPCA threatening to suspend our accreditation."

"The American Society for the Prevention of Cruelty to Animals?" asked Mrs. Pilfer.

"No," Hamhock corrected. "The Animal Society for Political Correctness in Academia. Much more strident."

The door rattled slightly, and everyone turned to see who might enter. But instead of an opening door, they witnessed a four-foot ball python slithering over the transom window and landing with the thud of an unsolicited manuscript.

"What news?" Sourgrapes asked.

Nora the python, special assistant to the president, had just come from the student meeting of FASC:ST, and she had much to report. She told the PUnC all that she had heard. How the cats had come together to take action and how others had joined them, including some professors. How the cat called Robespierre was their leader and how he was outraged by the whole M-word episode. How the cat called Chiffon had doubled down on everything Robespierre said and how the professor called Buck had advocated for a "focused, well-considered plan," rather than just "lashing out." Having no hands or fingers, Nora made "air quotes" by flicking her forked tongue on either side of the word she meant to emphasize.

"They ended their meeting," the python said, "by watching the video of the one called Socks. I must say that I really didn't get much out of it." Nora missed most of the video because ball pythons have poor eyesight and, although she could differentiate between live animals based on their infra-red signatures, the signal on the computer screen was just a hot, red rectangle to Nora, which did not allow her to discern shapes within the screen. And since ball pythons "hear" by receiving vibrations through their jaw bones, she couldn't catch much of what Socks was saying unless she had actually rested her jaw on the computer's speakers. As far as spying on her fellow animals went, Nora's great gift was that she could approach almost anyone without their knowledge by silently sidewinding up to them. If she got close enough and remained undetected, she was a great gatherer of intel.

"At the end of the video," Nora finished, "the two Jack Russells burst into the meeting to report on everything the dogs had been saying and doing," which she then also reported to the president and Provost.

"Very good," Sourgrapes said. "This is helpful. But how can we use it to solve our two bigger issues? Number *one*," he said with emphasis, "protecting the cats' feelings so they don't drop out. And number *two*, how do we keep our accreditation?"

On hearing these numbers, Mrs. Pilfer made a mad dash for the door. Among the experiments that researchers had inflicted upon her was training the rat to evacuate on command. This did not mean evacuating the building, as she currently found herself doing, but evacuating her bladder (number 1) and bowels (number 2) whenever she heard the numbers one and two. Now and again, on hearing those numbers outside the lab, she still felt a sudden and uncontrollable urge. This time she barely made it into the quad in time to "do the numbers" there. The whole thing might have been very embarrassing.

Blushing, Mrs. Pilfer returned to the president's office and went straight to the supply closet where she pulled out a large sheet of blank, rolled-up paper. Laying it on the floor, she unfurled it like a treasure map. Without saying a word, only occasionally pressing her front hands onto an inkpad, she began to render a complex diagram, with dozens of squares and circles and triangles, which she connected by lines that led from one shape to the next, sometimes with lines crossing other lines and sometimes with lines heading back to the beginning. The pig and the python looked on with confused expressions, but the fox immediately recognized what the rat was doing.

"Mind map," Sourgrapes said, as his mouth formed a smile. Mrs. Pilfer smiled back at him.

"Mind map?" Hamhock inquired.

"Yes," answered Sourgrapes. "We used to employ these during fox hunts to develop a strategy that would confuse the hounds and horses."

He then pointed to Pilfer's mind map and showed how each box (problem) might have lines joining it to other problems, but these had lines with arrows that led to triangles (action steps), which led to circles (solutions), which sometimes led to other problems, and so on. One path on Pilfer's mind map began with a square with "Socks" written inside. This led to a series of squares marked "Students" and "Faculty," with some of those having smaller, adjoining squares labeled "FASC:ST" and "PUnC," and others bearing specific names of particular cats or dogs or other animals. The triangles had words like "Investigate" and "Trial" written inside them, while the few circles on the mind map had words like "Banish" and "Accreditation." With his pointy black snout acting as a pointer, Sourgrapes followed every path, every divergence, every return to "home base." The final path could well have been labeled "way out of this mess." Mrs. Pilfer's mind map was elegant, if you knew how to read it, yet the convoluted arrows leading this way and that gave the appearance of a busy-ness that might lead to chaos, except for one word in a large circle in the middle. "Clarity" was all it said.

"Yes," Sourgrapes said. "This just might work."

Besides, the vulpine president thought, *it's a plan that leaves no fingerprints.* This was an odd thing to think, since—excepting chimps, gorillas, and, of all things, koalas—most mammals did not have fingerprints. (Any other animal might have said that their plan left no trace of a scent.) No matter. President Sourgrapes loved how the plan could not be traced back to him.

CHAPTER 6

Every day at 3pm sharp, the animals took a break from their academic work for *Nachmittagsfutterpause*. The phrase had originated with a silver-grey Weimaraner named Günther, a philosophy professor who, as the humans say, "has crossed the rainbow bridge." Günther would have been appalled by the use of such a phrase. He was dead, for dog's sake. Why mythologize and sugarcoat it?

Günther's thoughts toward religion echoed his attitude about the dignity of all animals. He believed it highly *un*dignified for creatures of higher intellectual capacity to participate in something as mundane as "afternoon feeding." So, he did what philosophers had always done and coined a neologism from a foreign language. In German, "afternoon feeding break," became *Nachmittagsfutterpause*, a collation of nouns, one joined to the next like some infinite centipede. The new word gave the concept an air of mystery, that "feeding" just didn't have. The few humans who still lingered at the college didn't understand the word, since humans had long ago stopped studying languages, which they considered impractical and of little use to the tasks that humans still performed. Using an obscure phrase for an activity as menial as eating also emphasized the privileged status of the animals.

The third Thursday of each month, *Nachmittagsfutterpause* occurred during the faculty meeting. This was by design since the Provost, herself a pig, realized that the best way to increase attendance at any meeting was to offer food. Amid the pecking, chomping, and chewing, the Provost hammered a tiny gavel against the wood floor of Reinvention Hall, where *Nachmittagsfutterpause*, and hence the faculty meeting, took place.

"Order, everyone. Order please." This never worked on the first attempt, so the Provost tried again. "Birds! Reptiles! Mammals! Please come to order!"

Animals slowly looked up from their water bowls and milk saucers and various feeding dishes. After the minutes from the last meeting and the agenda for this meeting were both approved, the Provost continued.

"I call upon Guinefort to offer the OINK."

The Opening Inspirational Nugget of Knowledge, or OINK, wasn't quite a prayer or invocation, since the animals didn't practice anything like religion. It was more like a reflection on the state of affairs at the college, given by a different faculty member at each meeting.

The room was packed with animal faculty, all of them focused on the greyhound as she approached the front of the room. Three of the pups—Groucho, Chico, and Harpo—continued to munch away. The pups weren't really on the faculty, but the college had no doggie day care, per se, and their dam was forced to bring them to the meeting. The two sister pups were nowhere in sight. Guinefort arrived at the front of the room.

"For gallantry," she said. "Gallantry!" She then recounted the story of Pwditat, a grey mackerel tabby from Hong Kong. When Pwditat was still a young kitten, she was taken aboard the HMS *Venture*, a British naval monitor, as a rat catcher. In 1949, communists attacked the *Venture* as she sailed up the Yangtze River. Many of the sailors on board were injured, as was Pwditat, who suffered burns and shrapnel wounds. Nonetheless, Pwditat soon resumed her rat catching duties, and also began visiting sick and wounded sailors. When Pwditat died, she was buried with full naval honors, including the award of the Dickin Medal for animal gallantry.

"Only 47 animals have received the Dickin since the end of World War II," Guinefort said. "These include 36 dogs, 8 pigeons, 2 horses, and one ship's cat: Pwditat."

Members of the faculty oohed and aahed at Guinefort's telling. Her words moved all who heard them, and the animals were hard pressed to remember when the OINK had been so poignant.

"This is inspiring," Guinefort continued, "and it's remarkable that this particular cat should be so honored. But this is also a story of anti-cat-ism. Of all the vessels in her majesty's royal navy—each one with a mouser or rat-catcher or two or three—only *one* cat ever received the Dickin! There is clearly species bias at work here, favoring dogs as recipients, as if dogs have the capacity for valor, but cats do not!"

Hmm, the animals collectively thought. The disparity had never occurred to them, but it made some sense when she put it that way.

"There's one more thing," Guinefort said, "but I'm nervous saying it. In fact, I'm just an adjunct and I could get fired by saying this, but ... Aesop College is an anti-cat-ite institution."

From the back of the room, Socks raised his head. That comment was meant for me, he thought. He decided to go on the offensive.

"You're right," he said. "Aesop College is anti-cat-ite. It has a species bias that favors dogs, just like the Dickin Medal. It also has biases against herbivores and piscivores, not to mention insectivores."

Many of the animals in the room furrowed their brows, puzzling over Sock's choice of vocabulary. Why didn't he just say, "plant eater, fish eater, bug eater?" they wondered. Who was he trying to impress?

"But you are not right about one thing, Guinefort. You are not right that anyone speaking the truth out loud can get fired. Academic freedom keeps that from happening."

"We'll see about that," she muttered under her breath.

"Colleagues," the Provost interrupted. "Please. Let's stick to the agenda." Socks backed down, but only after he and Guinefort exchanged some growls through clenched teeth. The Provost pretended to ignore the exchange.

"First on the agenda is curriculum reform. I believe we have a report from Professors Peeps."

The Velveteen Lop hopped to the podium, followed by Babette, the French Angora, who held several placards in her teeth.

"Thank you, Provost Hamhock," Peeps said. "We are here representing the Curriculum Reform and Oversight Committee, the CROC. First, I want to thank everyone on the committee." Peeps then proceeded to name everyone on the CROC, which consisted of almost every animal on the faculty, and one human, who acted as a consultant (though no one knew what that was), who could not be at today's faculty meeting because her human child had something called "soccer practice" and it was her turn to transport the young to their event.

"I have a PowerPoint," Peeps continued. "Let me just take a moment to set it up ..." There was some suppressed groaning in the crowd. "Oh, these things never work right away. Oh, sorry, sorry, sorry ..."

A rabbit PowerPoint was not the *son et lumière* that humans have come to expect when their colleagues use technology in their presentations. A rabbit PowerPoint consisted of a rabbit, in this case Professor Babette, who stood up on her hind legs and raised her ears to form an inverted easel, on which they rested several placards covered with text and graphs and other information. Thus balancing the placards, Babette removed them one by one, in a manner

Aesop's College 73

"I have a PowerPoint," Peeps said.

that resembled a kind of lapine burlesque dance. For his part, Professor Peeps held a small metal clicker in the shape of a frog. He would press down on the clicker's metal tongue, releasing a clear "clik-clok" as a signal to advance to the next slide.

The first placard, the obligatory "title slide," showed a picture of kittens playing with yarn. Several members of the faculty made cooing sounds and uttered such phrases as "how adorable," etc., though they puzzled over how the image might be connected to the content. At the bottom of the placard, rendered in the excellent if somewhat extravagant penmanship for which all rabbits are known, was the following:

> (AARD) VARK
> A New Approach to Teaching for a New Generation of Learners: How to Reach the Visual, Auditory, Reading, and Kinesthetic Student
>
> — Prof. Peeps, ARBA BOB
> Psychology Dept., Aesop College

"To begin," Peeps said, "I must thank Professor Babette in the Department of Human Languages for coming up with the acronym for this program." Babette lowered her head to cover her blushing, almost causing the placards to tumble from between her ears.

"As you all know, an aardvark is a type of ant-eater. The name comes from the Dutch. *Aard* means 'earth,' and *vark* means 'pig.' An aardvark is literally an 'earth-pig.'" Peeps chuckled at his own cleverness and looked to the Provost, who smiled her approval. "So, you see, (AARD)VARK is both a mnemonic and an acronym in one. Just remember 'aardvark' and you'll remember the four learning styles in VARK: visual, auditory, reading, and kinesthetic."

Clik-clok!

Babette reached up and removed the title slide, revealing the placard beneath. It showed three species of animal, each performing a task that seemed foreign to its nature: a rabbit chasing a Frisbee, a cat swimming, a dog flapping two palm fronds in the air attempting to fly.

"This has been our pedagogical method for far too long," Peeps said, pointing to the placard with a long carrot that he had suddenly produced. "We used to force students to learn things that they really had no innate ability to do."

"Is this why so many of our students fail?" a voice from the faculty shouted out.

"We don't like to think of our students as failures," Peeps said. "We prefer to think of them as 'deferred successes.' But it *is* the reason students complain that they have to learn things they'll never use." Peeps went on to explain the significance of (AARD)VARK's system of pedagogy. How students didn't really fail at learning so much as teachers failed at teaching. How the best teachers adapted their teaching to each individual student's learning style.

"Every student is special," said Peeps. "Therefore, every student must have a special learning style. There's visual." Here Peeps emphatically gestured toward his PowerPoint. "Aural." Here he clicked the clicker—clik-clok!—which he meant as a sound effect, but which confused Professor Babette into advancing to the next placard, which Peeps had to correct. "Reading," Peeps said, at which point he turned his back on the crowd of animals, looked up at the PowerPoint and began to move his head from side to side, reading the words on the slide in pantomime. "And kinesthetic," he said, and hopped to and fro.

Clik-clok!

Babette revealed a placard with a bar graph showing comparative GPAs, before and after adopting (AARD) VARK.

Clik-clok!

Another placard showed the distribution of learning styles across all species.

Clik-clok!

The final placard held an easy 25-point plan for implementation over a 5-year period.

The faculty asked many questions, but all of them had the same format. They began with praise for the CROC.

"Thank you all so much for your work. You've really put a lot of effort into this." These preambles, some of them quite lengthy, were designed to put the committee members at ease, to deflect the full impact of the question at hand, which was never really a question at all, but a statement disguised as a question that was meant to disparage the committee's plan. Buck, the Rottweiler, stood to speak.

"What a great job you rabbits have done. We're all so grateful. But what about the inter-species application of this program?"

"The program is designed—" Peeps began.

"Isn't it true," Buck continued, "that a *rogue* professor, with his own political program, could implement VARK on the surface, but, in reality, promote his own agenda? Like reading ant-cat-ite texts to the consternation of cats?"

"Okay," said Socks. "I've just about had it with—"

"With what?" Buck snapped at Socks and bared his fangs. Even though the Rottweiler was twice his size, the border collie bared his fangs, too, and they both growled their fiercest growls. Buck immediately moved to Socks's side and pushed his head into Socks's shoulder, forming a T-shape with their two bodies. His hackles were raised and he scratched the ground. Buck was ready to grab Socks by the scruff of the neck if he did not submit. Socks turned his head to face Buck, a little too abruptly and within seconds they had engaged. Barking, biting, scratching. Guinefort jumped into the fray and nipped at Socks's heels, until Jake and Argos came to the aid of their friend and butted her out of the way. The rabbits and other prey animals shrank away to the walls in the room. Professor Babette fell backwards and the PowerPoint placards dispersed to the four winds. At last, the Provost made a loud squealing noise, which distracted all the animals just long enough for them to hear Hamhock once again banging her gavel.

"Please!" the Provost shouted. "Please. This isn't kosher! Remember *Rabbit's Rules of Order*!"

Animals froze in place, paws poised to strike, postures ready to leap, looking with wide eyes over their shoulders at the Provost. Their poses resembled the empty shells of animals live-cast in lava at the eruption of Mount Vesuvius in the first century AD.

As calm slowly returned, those petrified in mid-brawl, panting heavily from the intense skirmish, could hear a distant chanting that grew louder with every tired breath they took. Cats and their allies were marching through the quad toward Reinvention Hall. The protestors reached the windows outside and the chant became clearer.

"THE FELINES, UNITED, WILL NEVER BE DIVIDED! THE FELINES, UNITED, WILL NEVER BE DIVIDED!"

All the animals chanted with gusto, regardless of species. The rabbits were among the loudest, holding neatly-lettered signs with slogans like "Hop to it, Hamhock!" and "If Socks is anti-cat-ite, then I prefer to go barefoot!" Zeppo and Gummo, the two female pups, marched with the cats, carrying a banner between them that read, "These bitches are angry!" Some kittens on the edges of the march wore T-shirts with "Pussy Power" scrawled across the front. Others wore buttons that said, "Resist the dominant food chain!"

President Sourgrapes, witnessing the growing protest from his office window, smiled as he saw that last one.

At the head of the group was Robespierre, his defiant, clenched paw in the air, waving a sign that read, "Question the taxonomic hierarchy!" Chiffon was right behind him with a sign covered in "Cute Little Kitty" stickers, with purple block letters reading "THE FUTURE IS FELINE!"

Once their numbers had filled the quad, they switched to a different chant:

"WHAT DO WE WANT?

"An end to species-ism and anti-cat-ite rhetoric in the classroom, and no more privileged professors protected under the guise of academic freedom!"

"WHEN DO WE WANT IT?

"NOW!" [*da capo*]

Waves of anger and exhilaration swept through the crowd. Provost Hamhock left the relative safety of Reinvention Hall to come into the quad and meet the protestors, while the animal faculty pressed their snouts and muzzles against the windows of the Hall to get a better look.

"Dear, dear students," the Provost said. "We hear you." She stood on her hind legs, trying to balance as she gestured with her front petittoes. "This has been a difficult week at Aesop College, and we want to make it right by you."

"Enough words!" one of the protestors shouted. "We want action!" There followed several more cat calls and barks from the crowd, mixed together so horribly as to make them indiscernible. In truth, it was Cindy and Cyndi, the Jack Russells, who were agitating the crowd from within.

"I understand," the pig said, by which she meant the emotions rather than the words. "And we do plan to take action."

"Fire Professor Socks!" came another anonymous screech. The crowd joined in. "FIRE SOCKS! FIRE SOCKS!"

"It's not as simple as that," said the Provost. "There's due process. And the matter of tenure. Things would have to be very serious to fire a tenured professor."

"How serious does it need to be?" It was Robespierre, who had momentarily put down his clenched fist, but still held on to his sign. "Socks is guilty of species-ism. He used the M-word in a classroom full of cats!"

"He hurt the students' feelings," Chiffon added with some urgency.

"Yes. I understand all that," the Provost began again, still hoping that reason and due process might rule the day. Her appeals were met with more chanting.

"HEY-HEY. HO-HO. PROFESSOR SOCKS HAS GOT TO GO. HEY-HEY. HO-HO. PROFESSOR SOCKS HAS GOT TO GO."

In the midst of this new round of chanting, a lithe figure the color of a blood orange with a black-tipped tail cut through the crowd from the rear. It was President Sourgrapes, who had seized upon the moment to address the protestors and enact his master plan, based on the mind map of Mrs. Pilfer.

"Students, students, students," said Sourgrapes. "Of course, we will take action. And of course, Socks will stand trial."

No one had yet mentioned a trial. The Provost scratched her head with her trotter, trying to remember if the faculty handbook had a procedure for putting a professor on trial. She rather thought that it did not.

"Of course, Professor Socks will be fired," Sourgrapes continued. "But first we must find him guilty with a jury of his peers." The fox president was as clever as any human administrator. His language was just obscure enough so that the audience would hear due process, if that's what they wanted to hear, or pandering to the mob, if that was their preference.

"I propose a trial in one week," the president said. "During which time, Professor Socks will remain in the doghouse and will not be allowed to teach." The Provost sat back on her haunches. The president had clearly taken charge of the situation and Hamhock recognized that no good could come from protesting this fact in public.

"I designate Provost Hamhock as the prosecutor, since she's most familiar with the case, and holds the most authority by virtue of her office." Here the fox paused and looked around the quad, but he could not see the faculty member he was looking for.

"Where is the law professor?" Sourgrapes asked, as if only remembering in that moment that a new young prof had recently joined the faculty. "Jack Flash? Is that his name?"

"Yes," said Hamhock. A call relayed its way like buckets in a fire brigade, from the quad to the inside of Reinvention Hall to the spot where Jack Flash, the kangaroo adjunct in law, was busy taking notes because someone had told him that that's what one should do at a faculty meeting. Once he received the president's request, the kangaroo jumped nervously over several of the smaller animals and presented himself to Sourgrapes in the front of the building. He bowed as low as he could out of deference, which was difficult, his being twice as tall as the fox.

"You will serve as the judge," said President Sourgrapes. He read the panic on the kangaroo's face but held up a paw to stop any objections. "No. You understand the law, even if you are still a graduate student. And since you're new to the community, you'll be unbiased in the matter. And even though you're only an adjunct, I want you to be honest and sincere in your judgments, knowing that nothing will happen to you, no matter how you rule."

One of the kittens with the "Pussy Power" T-shirts raised her paw to ask a question. Sourgrapes smiled. Plan initiated, he thought. And once again, no fingerprints.

CHAPTER 7

The week passed slowly. Provost Hamhock prepped witnesses and organized the evidence for the prosecution. Jack Flash reviewed law cases and legal precedents. The entire Aesop community was abuzz, including the bees.

For his part, Socks pondered the long legal history concerning animals and animals on trial and sank into a deep depression.

The Laws of Eshnunna in ancient Mesopotamia (c.1930 BC) asserted that if one ox gored and killed another, the owner of the killer ox would pay the owner of the dead ox half the sum of the value of both oxen. This was an attempt at an economic solution that tried to give both owners something close to the value of their property. But if an ox was known to have gored before and then killed a human, the ox owner would have to pay two-thirds a *mina* of silver (whatever that was) to the dead human's family. This was the same fine levied against a dog that killed a human, if the dog was known to be a biter. Of course, if the ox or dog only killed a slave, the price was just 15 *shekels*. (Not sure what a *shekel* was, but pretty sure it was a lot less than a *mina*.) Since animals were seen as property—just as slaves were—legal issues were resolved in economic terms. The more famous Code of Hammurabi (c. 1754 BC) took a similar stance in its laws about animals but went into greater detail. For example, Hammurabi's code not only set the prices for humans gored to death by oxen (more for free men, less for slaves), it also regulated the rental price of oxen and resolved liability issues

Jack Flash reviewed law cases and legal precedents.

between the renter and the owner in cases where oxen were killed while on duty—especially by lions.

It wasn't until the ancient Hebrews adapted some of these laws (after the Babylonian Captivity) that morality began to be applied to animals. For example, Exodus 21:28-32 employed great legalistic detail to parse the matter of the goring ox. According to this passage, if an ox gored someone to death, the ox was stoned and no one should eat of its flesh, a punishment that clearly signaled an inherent evil in the ox.

Aristotle and Plato spoke of trials against animals, most often for animals that had killed humans, but these were no different than the trials against inanimate objects! Apparently, trials in ancient Greece had the goal of restoring moral equilibrium to any city-state, or *polis*, that had been disturbed by the murder of one of its citizens. If the animal (or object) were not put on trial, the avenging spirit of the victim might bring plagues, droughts, and other misfortunes upon the *polis*.

Things didn't get truly nutty until the animal trials of the Middle Ages. Such trials were divided into two types: ecclesiastical and civil.

The ecclesiastical courts dealt mainly with wild animals, especially those that were difficult to capture and kill, that caused a public nuisance effecting the greater community. For example, the Church might intervene to bring divine justice against a swarm of locusts that was destroying the local crops. According to medieval court documents, church officials "compelled the locusts to desist from their devastations and to retire from all places devoted to the production of human sustenance." Usually, three or four sample locusts would be brought to court and ritually stomped on as church officials pronounced the anathema against their locust brethren.

The secular, civil courts dealt with animals that caused injury or death to individual humans. Such trials were only possible because the animals were domesticated and could more easily be arrested and detained for trial. The community provided accused animals with defense counsel, free of charge, and these lawyers advocated for their clients with all the rigor they had, as if the defendants were human. For example, in 1540, in the infamous case of the rats of Autun—who were subpoenaed to appear before a judge for allegedly eating the community's barley crop—defense counsel Bartholomé Chassenée argued that the rats had not been given proper notice or time to appear, that the subpoena for their appearance had not been distributed widely enough, and that some of the rats feared appearing in court because many of the plaintiffs in the case had "evil-disposed cats," who might harm the rats on the way to court. Abiding by Chassenée's argument, the court required the plaintiffs to post bonds for their cats to ensure that they did no harm to the rats, at which point the plaintiffs gave up and dropped their complaint. Chassenée gained such fame in the case that he advanced to high office in the royal government.

Animals could sometimes become witnesses in human trials. For example, in 16th-century Switzerland, a defendant accused of murdering an intruder in his house claimed self-defense and was allowed to produce a dog as a witness. Since the dog (saying nothing) did not contradict the defendant's claim, the accused was found not guilty.

Animals occasionally got caught up in the crimes and sins of humans. For example, in Chartres in 1606, a man was hanged for practicing sodomy with a female canine. In one of the first cases of "blaming the victim," the bitch was burned at the stake. Human judges sometimes granted mercy to animal victims, as in the case of a farmer sodomizing his donkey in 15th-century Italy. The farmer was hanged, but the donkey was acquitted and freed from any burdensome work for its remaining days.

Socks was aware that, in human trials, some races were found guilty more often than others. Such prejudice also played itself out in animal trials. Pigs seemed especially susceptible. For example, a pig was hanged for infanticide in 1386 in Normandy and again in 1394 in Aquitaine, while in 1408 in Burgundy, a pig was merely imprisoned for eating a child. Burgundy must have had good lawyers, for in 1379, two herds of swine in that region received pardons for murder because only three of them were actually guilty.

The strangest case of porcine prosecution involved the so-called "savage pigs of Tulla." In 18th-century Ireland, a farmer had imbibed too much whiskey before returning from market with two sows to his small farm in the village of Tulla. He fell asleep at the reins of his wagon, then toppled backward into the cart, where the pig proceeded to eat him. The cart horse, for her part, knew the way back to the farm and didn't stop till it got home. By the time the farmer's wife discovered the cart parked by the front gate, the only remains of the farmer were two boney stumps sticking out of his boots. The wife called her neighbors and the vicar, and a great debate ensued over what to do next. The poor farmers were in the middle of a famine. To try the pigs for murder and hang or burn them as punishment seemed a terrible waste. Yet to eat the pigs seemed akin to cannibalism, since parts of the farmer were still inside them. And what of the farmer's soul? Had it left his body at the moment of his death? Or was it still inside the pigs? The villagers ended up burying the pigs, in their entirety, in the local churchyard. A stone marker with two pigs carved into it sits atop the grave to this day.

Socks pondered how often religion played a part in these animal trials and recalled the case of the rooster tried in Basel in 1474 for "the heinous and unnatural crime of laying an egg," which the villagers believed was caused by Satan.

Ignorant, superstitious humans, thought Socks.

Yet humans did occasionally display some insight and mercy regarding their fellow mammals—even if they still behaved badly toward the fish and fowl. For example, Leonardo Da Vinci was a vegetarian and spoke out against cock fighting and bear baiting. Thomas More in his *Utopia* advocated for mercy toward all of God's creatures, while the French Renaissance philosopher Montaigne saw animals as morally equivalent to humans. (Or was it the other way around?) English philosopher and social reformer Jeremy Bentham argued that animals deserved better treatment because they had feelings. According to Bentham, "The question is not, 'Can they reason?' nor, 'Can they talk?' but, 'Can they suffer?'" Liliana Carnevale, the human student who had started the movement to give the college over to its comfort animals, would have approved.

With all of these historic animal trials swirling in his mind, Socks was surprised to realize that his trial would be the first in history in which animals put one of their own on trial. Yet it was hard for him to marvel at the novelty of the moment, since his own future as a professor and as a member of the community were at stake. The atmosphere on Aesop's campus became so unwelcoming that Socks had little desire to return. It felt as if everyone was against him.

Indeed, members of Aesop's faculty had many questions and opinions about Sock's situation and the impending trial. What had actually happened? What did it all mean? Did the Provost have the authority to take Socks to trial? Was it sanctioned in the Animal Faculty Handbook? Could the trial lead to Socks's dismissal? Could he be put to death?

"I think the Provost is overreaching," Argos said to a group of dogs during *Nachmittagsfutterpause*. "The *faculty* should be deciding whether Socks did anything wrong in the classroom."

"I think he should appeal to the president," said Jake.

"No, no, no," one of the rabbits insisted. "You have to respect the food chain."

"That's an odd statement coming from someone at the 'prey' end of the continuum."

The President and Provost received harsh letters of criticism from People United for Animal Academics, the PUAA, a human advocacy group that defended the rights of academic freedom for mammalian professors. The incident even received national attention, with stories published in *Cat Fancy* and *Modern Dog* magazines, and a twenty-minute investigative piece on the television show "Animal World." Human "dog whisperers" and canine behaviorists offered commentary on daytime talk shows.

"Can anything be done to stop canine professors from using the M-word?" the host would ask.

"Oh, of course," a smarmy dog whisperer would reply. "It will take patience, but with Skinnerian methods of biofeedback and behavior modification, even the most stubborn dog can be reprogrammed so that they themselves experience revulsion over using such terms."

"These are deep-seated prejudices," a trained animal psychologist would offer. "This level of anti-cat-ism is a sign of puppyhood trauma, such as loud noises from fireworks on national holidays, being removed from the litter too soon, or being left alone for too long. Any of these could contribute to species-ism that may never be overcome."

Then there were the dark forces of true species-ism, the alt-right animal haters who promoted the most outrageous anti-cat-ite speakers just to get a rise out of animals on the left, so that those on the right could claim to be the real champions of free speech and academic freedom.

"Can you believe what's happening at Aesop College?" they would shout into their AM talk radio microphones or type in ALL CAPS on their conservative blogs. "A canine professor was yanked from the classroom because he read a word, as written, from a famous poem! I mean *really*! These whiny cats seem more like possums that roll over and pretend to die at the first hint of anything that upsets them!"

One commentator labeled them "animal snowflakes." Another called them "social justice fourriers (from an Old French word for foragers).

"If a gathering of buzzards is called a wake," quipped a late-night comedian, "is a gathering of liberal animals a 'woke?'"

The entire Aesop community was astounded at how much attention this isolated incident on their small campus was attracting.

One student, a cat who had been in Socks's class that day, left a note for the professor in the storm drain where he was known to sleep. Here's what it said:

Dear Prof. Sox,
    I can't believe the treatment you've gotten because of comments you made during class. Your words were taken completely out of context and my fellow cats on the left attacked without cause. As you probably know, this is happening at college campuses across the country and I think it's tearing at the seams of free speech.
    You're not an anti-cat-ite, I don't care what the clowder mob is calling you. Lots of students agree with you, even cats, but like me, they're too afraid to step forward for risk of being condemned by their peers. This is the problem with the toxic southpaws. They throw around words like "species-ism" and "anti-cat-ite" like they're death sentences. I know you don't want to lose your job. I know it'd be easier to apologize. I know you're being swept up in this "liberal" reactionary wave.
    I'm not a conservative. I'd even say I hold more liberal values. But it's the radical southpaws that are

getting good people fired for no real reason other than being "triggered." It makes me sick to my stomach!

I'm ashamed that I have to ask you this, but please keep this note between you and me. I can't risk having my friends find out.

[Name withheld,]

Socks sank into a deep depression.

In spite of all the accomplishments animals had made, it was still illegal for them to buy alcohol. Hence, on several nights that week, Socks hung out at student bars on the edge of Bigg State University, lapping up beer that students had spilled on the sidewalk. One night he was so bummed out that he even ate the vomit of an inebriated frat boy, hoping that the student had wretched up enough alcohol to get him drunk.

When the day of the trial arrived, the animals gathered once again in Reinvention Hall. Holding the trial in the quad would have been better in terms of allowing more animals to view the proceedings, but maximum audience was not the goal. Hamhock and Sourgrapes decided that the fewer animals to see what was happening, the better. This would reduce the number of objections during the trial and if animals chose to object after the fact, it was easy to dismiss their concerns by pointing out that the complainers "hadn't been there" or "didn't have all the information."

Reinvention Hall was outfitted to resemble the set of a television courtroom drama. Aesop College only had one working television that very few of the animals ever watched. Guinefort, however, had developed a near addiction to these courtroom dramas back when she was still living with humans and she had taken some time to make sure the "courtroom" for Socks's trial had the right look. At one end of the room, Guinefort arranged the highest lab desk she could find on top of four cinder blocks, to make it even higher. This would be the judge's bench. Next to the bench, she put a much lower swivel chair. It had a cushiony seat and wooden arm rests. This would be the witness stand. Next to this, she roped off an area where the jury would sit, though she didn't know how many jurors there would be, so she left the area without any chairs. She placed a long cafeteria table across from the judge's bench and a little to the right. This would be the prosecutor's table. Next to this and slightly to the left of the bench, she placed a tablet arm desk with metal legs, an orange poly shell seat, and a flat, laminated tablet top attached to an arm that came up on one side. The angle of the desktop was just steep enough that papers easily slid off. This was the desk assigned to Socks, who had chosen to serve as his own defense counsel—*pro se*, as the humans say.

As a finishing touch, on the wall behind the judge's bench, Guinefort painted a copy of the college seal that stood above the main door of Reinvention Hall. The seal was in the shape of a circle. Around its edges, the school's Latin motto read as follows: "*Lepus cerebrum—Mens testudo*" across the top, and "*Omnes educandi*" across the bottom.

It's a shame I never learned Spanish, Guinefort thought to herself, yet all the same she copied the letters as accurately as she could. The center of the seal showed two figures, a hare in the foreground with a tortoise following behind, illustrating Aesop's best-known fable, which Guinefort and all the animals at the school knew and understood very well.

Buck stood by the entrance to the Reinvention Hall. He had been assigned as the court bailiff and his first task was to monitor who would and would not be admitted to the trial. The first group he allowed in were nine cats of various breeds, none of whom had been party to the events in Socks's classroom. This was the jury. There were no chairs or cushions of any kind in the jury box and the cats began to fill the space by pacing back and forth. A couple of them jumped up on the windowsill, then back down again. Several of them moved in and out of the area that Guinefort had roped off and it took some convincing from Buck to keep them all within the bounds of the rope.

Buck then allowed Mrs. Pilfer to enter. She would act as the court recorder. A laptop had been set up on the floor in front of the judge's bench and she took her place there. Next came Provost Hamhock, who would serve as the prosecutor. She laid out copies of witness statements and other bits of evidence, among them her first edition of *Old Possum's Book of Practical Cats*, as well as several blank notepads, on the long cafeteria table, to be ready when the trial began. Socks then entered. He had no brief case and nary a document. He hopped up on the tablet arm desk that Guinefort had provided and assumed a relaxed pose, front legs crossed on the desktop.

The last one to enter was the fox, Reynaldo Sourgrapes, who took a place in the gallery. He was the only inside observer of the trial, a decision he himself had made, unbeknownst to anyone else. All other observers had to pile up in the quad and hope for a view through the windows of Reinvention Hall. Once the president had been seated, Buck walked behind the bench and knocked on the door of a broom closet in one corner of the room. This served as the judge's chambers, from which emerged the honorable kangaroo, Jack Flash.

"ALL RISE!" Buck barked.

Mrs. Pilfer was the first to her feet, followed by Provost Hamhock. The cats in the jury box all stood, but they did not stand still, weaving betwixt each other's bodies. Socks didn't stand, but instead raised his head slightly and turned to look behind himself. There, President Sourgrapes sat. definitely not standing.

"COURT IS NOW IN SESSION! THE RIGHT HONORABLE JUDGE JACK FLASH (*locum tenens pro tempore*) PRESIDING."

Judge Flash hopped out of the closet carrying several unwieldy legal tomes and wearing a black silk bathrobe that Guinefort had found in what remained of the college's human "lost & found" bin. It was too long for Flash's torso, but it would have to do as a judge's robe. Jack Flash hopped over the stool behind his desk several times, back and forth, the robe fluttering behind him like some superhero's cape, until he finally hopped up onto the bench, then down onto the stool. Once he'd settled in, Flash organized the law books he had brought in front of him. There was the Roman *Corpus juris civilis* as well as the law codes of Justinian and Theodosius. The Napoleonic code was there, as was the German civil code embodied in the *Bürgerliches Gesetzbuch*. Finally, he laid out the mimeographed pages of Title 18 of the United States Penal Code, Part II, which deals with criminal procedure. Noticeably absent from the bench was any copy of the Aesop Faculty Handbook.

"BE SEATED," barked Buck. And they were.

"Right," said Jack Flash. "We'll begin with opening arguments."

"Gullinburst Hamhock for the prosecution, your honor." The pig rose and approached the jury box.

"Honorable felines," she continued. "Your job today is an important one. Not only must you determine the guilt or innocence of Professor Socks, who is charged with willfully uttering words that have caused grave injury to our students. No. Much greater than that, your actions today, your decisions, your judgment, will determine the kind of school Aesop will be to future students, whether or not Aesop College will uphold the highest standards of the academic community and punish those who use forbidden language, or allow animals who should know better to denigrate our standards for their own intellectual entertainment, doing serious harm to our students in the process.

"The prosecution will show that Professor Socks did read from a book of human poetry and in so doing did utter aloud a word that should never be uttered. Even now as I speak to you, I can only employ a euphemism, the 'M-word,' so vile is the actual word to cats, and indeed all creatures who have any sense of decency. Socks used the M-word in class, terrorizing our young students—cats just like yourselves—and then went on to discuss whether or not its use could ever be justified, clearly deciding for himself that it could be, in spite of well-worn community standards."

The cats in the jury box were uncharacteristically focused on the Provost's words, as if Hamhock were dangling a toy mouse in front of them.

"Yes. He did all of these things and worse: he refused to apologize after the fact. Not once did we see Socks with his head hung low, eyes pleading, slinking across the campus with his tail between his legs. He has offered not a single sign of contrition or remorse. In fact, he seems proud to have said this forbidden word in class, and even prouder not to apologize for doing so! What kind of *animal* is he?

"Instead he speaks of academic freedom, as if that were the highest value of the academy! He has rallied those in the public square against us, disparaging Aesop College as a place where academic freedom doesn't live. This is an outrage! Academic freedom is alive and well at Aesop College, but we believe this freedom must extend to our students' right not to hear certain teachings that might damage them. This is what Professor Socks has done, and he must be called to task."

One of the cats on the jury started to applaud, which caused a couple of the other cats to follow suit. Judge Flash threw a stern look and hammered his gavel to indicate that this behavior was not appropriate.

"Finally, members of the jury, I urge you to use caution when evaluating this case. Professor Socks will also present his side of things and I advise you ... use caution. Border collies are among the smartest species on earth. But do not be fooled by his words, do not be taken in by his rhetoric. Socks has a way, as the ancient humans used to say, of 'making the worst argument into the best argument.' He has ways of speaking, techniques of argumentation, that may convince you to adopt his point of view, even though he himself is no expert on the matter. So, beware!"

Hamhock walked back to the long table, casting an accusatory eye on Socks as she did. For his part, Socks remained seated for what felt like minutes before he stood to address the jury. He walked slowly to one corner of the jury box, sat down and tilted his head as he made eye contact with each and every jury member, calling them by name.

"Bella. Simba. Chloe. Nala. Smokey. Tigger Number Three. Shadow. Willow. Romeo. It's been some time since I've seen all of you. I was in school with some of you. Some of you I had as students. Some of you I only know because you're members of our community. But we all know each other."

The cats in the jury began to purr.

"Or perhaps we don't know each other—at least not as well as I'd like—but we would certainly recognize each other, walking across the quad or prowling the neighborhood. It's odd, though, that I barely recognize myself from the vivid but dubious description given by my esteemed colleague, the Provost."

Socks began to pace in front of the jury box and the cats leaned in, their ears forward and their eyes focused, trying to catch his meaning.

"The Provost says that your duty is much greater than determining my guilt or innocence. I agree. I also agree that your verdict will cast the future of Aesop College, as a school of unchanging truth, or a school that bends to the whims of the moment."

Socks made a dismissive gesture with his paw as he said, "whims of the moment."

"The Provost says that I read from a book of human poetry and that I said a word out loud that shouldn't be said out loud. I've never denied this. But two questions come from this. The first is the context in which I said the word and how that context makes a difference. The second is the relationship of academic freedom to what the Provost calls 'community standards' and whether, in a free society, there are *any* words that can *never* be said."

The cats in the jury box looked at each other as if they were really pondering this question.

"The Provost says that I refused to apologize for my actions after the fact. On one level, this simply isn't true. I apologized. The question is whether that apology was sincere and why the students refused to accept it."

At this point in Socks's opening argument, Hamhock let loose a loud fart, which was perfectly normal behavior for a pig in any other venue, but in the pomp and circumstance of the courtroom it seemed untoward. Socks glared at the Provost, then looked to the kangaroo sitting at the bench. The judge simply shrugged, as if to say, "This was biology, not commentary," but Socks was unconvinced. Nonetheless, he continued.

"The Provost says ... the Provost says that I've defended academic freedom. Yes. And I would do it again and again and ever more. It's the currency of the professoriate, a principle that makes us more than mere animals, and one that protects all professors, not just the so-called 'privileged canines.' Academic freedom also protects students, though not in the way that the Provost would have you believe, by protecting them from hearing hard truths. No. Academic freedom allows students to protest those uncomfortable truths, but it does not allow them to silence Truth. Academic freedom protects students and professors and indeed the

Provost herself, even when they speak out against academic freedom. But academic freedom cannot silence academic freedom."

Socks had them eating out of his paw.

"Finally, the Provost accuses me of 'making the worst argument into the best argument.'"

Here Socks gestured air quotes with his front paws.

"But this is an old rhetorical trick that the Provost knows only too well, one that's always used to disparage a speaker and *sow* doubt in the listeners' minds." Here, Socks tossed in his own rhetorical trick. Rather than pronounce "sow" to rhyme with "so," as in "sowing seeds," he made it rhyme with "cow," to indicate a female pig, a "sow." Fewer than half the cats picked up on this, but the ones who did smiled at the professor's clever turn of phrase. Hamhock definitely caught the *jeu de mots* but couldn't decide whether to smile or scowl.

"Frankly," Socks continued, "I'm almost stunned the Provost hasn't charged me with 'corrupting the youth.'"

President Sourgrapes caught the reference and let out a huge guffaw from the gallery, then covered his muzzle with his paws to stop himself.

"The Provost asks you to be wary and not to be fooled. And I say the same. Much is at stake here."

There was a long moment of silence in the courtroom. The cats in the jury were motionless, which is saying a lot. The Provost was gobsmacked. She stared at Socks, half forgetting her accusation that Socks was capable of making the worst argument into the best. If that's what just happened, Hamhock thought, it was a *tour de force*.

From the bench, *locum tenens pro tempore* Judge Jack Flash struck his gavel with authority and pronounced:

"The prosecution shall call its first witness."

CHAPTER 8

"CALL THE FIRST WITNESS!" Buck shouted.

"The prosecution calls Magda the cat," said the Provost.

Outside in the quad, animals had been stacked three high atop one another, trying to see into the courtroom. Nora the python was on her perch in the crux of the old elm. High above her was the crow named Lucifer, the bringer of light. A mad scurrying began on hearing Magda's name. The entire crowd had watched the opening arguments of each side with rapt attention, even those who were not raptors.

"Magda the cat," someone said. "They're asking for Magda." The grey Persian squeezed her way through the crowd and entered Reinvention Hall. Buck opened the door and pointed her toward the witness stand. Once Magda was seated, Buck pointed to a can of tuna, perched on a velvet pillow, atop a small pedestal.

"Place your paw on the tuna and repeat after me," Buck said. "Hey diddle diddle, the cat and the fiddle. The cow jumped over the moon. The little dog laughed to see such a sight and the dish ran away with the spoon."

Magda began to repeat the verse, but then her face took on a confused look. She had never been to court, much less sworn an oath like this. And while she had heard this nursery rhyme many times before, she had no idea why it should be included in her oath to give honest testimony. The judge, who was really just a kangaroo grad student in law, offered an explanation.

"Place your paw on the tuna and repeat after me."

"The cat and the fiddle," Flash said, "is a corruption of the Latin *cattus fidelis*, i.e., the faithful cat. The cow jumping over the moon refers to the constellation of Taurus during a blue moon, i.e., the fourth full moon in a season of three full moons. During such an event, it literally looks as if Taurus is 'jumping' over the moon. The ancients believed that this celestial omen required absolute honesty on the part of anyone making a promise or swearing an oath. The 'little dog laughing' refers to *Canis major*, the Dog Star, which is also prominent in the night sky when the cow does its jumping. Since dogs symbolize fidelity and honesty, the little dog laughs because, during this time, all the other creatures of the earth are held to the same high standard of truth that he is."

"What about the dish 'running away' with the spoon?" asked Magda.

"An excellent question," said grad student in law and judge *pro tempore* Jack Flash. "This symbolizes famine, the food dish literally running away. It represents the wrath of nature toward anyone not telling the truth."

"Oh," Magda said. It was more explanation than she had expected and the whole thing still seemed silly to her. She finished the verse and began grooming her lush fur for self-comfort. Provost Hamhock, prosecutor, approached the witness stand.

"Please state your name and occupation for the record." Magda looked stunned, as if anyone could possibly not know her name.

"Magda," she finally said. "I'm a student here."

"Now, Magda. Where were you on the day in question?"

"In Professor Socks's class on 20th-century poets."

"And do you recall what happened in that class?"

"He used the M-word."

"And how did that make you feel?"

"It was horrible! All of the cats felt as if they were being attacked! I don't even want to think of it ..."

Magda continued her description of the horrors in Socks's class for several minutes. When prompted to cross examine the witness, Socks declined. The Provost called her next witness, the Abyssinian, Cleopatra.

Hey diddle diddle, etc.

"Please state your name."

"Cleopatra."

"Where were you on the day in question?"

"In Professor Socks's class ... he used the M-word ... it was horrible ..."

Socks again declined the opportunity to cross-examine the witness, so Hamhock called the next one.

"Chiffon ... In Professor Socks's class ..."

Before Chiffon could finish her testimony, Socks stood and addressed the bench.

"Your honor, the defense recognizes that my esteemed colleague for the prosecution has lined up a string of witnesses—Chiffon, Robespierre, Tiny Tim, and others—all of whom will testify that they were in my class on the day in question and that they heard me say the M-word, a fact which I have never denied and to which we will stipulate without having to hear all of this testimony. The defense also stipulates that all of these witnesses had their feelings hurt, that they found the experience of hearing this word harmful and horrifying, that they cannot believe it happened, *et cetera, et cetera*. We do not contest the feelings of these witnesses, largely because feelings are not facts, and in a court of law, facts are what matters. So, in the interest of time, I move that their testimony, such as it is, be entered into the record uncontested."

"Objections?" the kangaroo said looking at the pig.

"None, your honor," replied the pig.

"If that's the entirety of the prosecution's case ..." Socks attempted, but Provost Hamhock cut him off.

"Oh, we have other witnesses who will bring other testimony into evidence."

"Proceed," said Flash.

"The prosecution calls Professor Peeps."

Peeps hopped onto the cushiony swivel chair that was the witness stand. Buck approached the rabbit to swear him in.

"No need for that can of tuna," Peeps said. "I don't believe in your traditions or superstitions. But rest assured that there is no more honest creature than a rabbit. So many of us having sacrificed our lives so that human women could find out if they were 'with child' ... it makes a species both honorable and candid."

Buck looked at the judge to see how to proceed, but the kangaroo waived him off.

"Professor Peeps," the Provost said. "Please state your full name for the record."

"Just Peeps."

"And your occupation?"

"I'm a psychology professor here at Aesop College."

"And your specialty?"

"I research the psychology of learning and pedagogy," Peeps said. "I have a PowerPoint that explains the discipline in great detail, if you like."

"No. Thank you. I'm sure that won't be necessary," the Provost replied and smiled as she saw Socks out of the corner of her eye giving a sigh of relief.

"Professor Peeps, explain to us the impact on students—the emotional, psychological impact—when students are traumatized in the classroom by the content being taught or the manner in which that content is presented."

"Certainly. Students exposed to traumatic images or language, especially in the dangerous environment of a classroom, may be triggered to experience emotions that cause them to shut down emotionally. This triggering can also happen if they think a professor is condescending, i.e., talking down to them, or if they perceive him to be mocking them by asking them difficult questions that they might not know the answers to, a practice that they call 'gas-lighting.' Of course, as teachers, shutting down is the last thing we want our students to do. It makes it impossible for any deep learning to take place."

"And would the 'M-word' be included in this list of 'triggering language'?"

"I don't like to think of it as a list, per se, but yes, the M-word is what we call a 'super trigger.'"

"Thank you, Professor Peeps. Nothing further at this time."

Hamhock returned to her seat, nodding toward Socks as she went, to indicate that Peeps was now his witness. Socks sat up on his hind legs and cocked his head to the right. He stayed that way for some time, considering how to approach his line of questioning. Suddenly, he found himself hopping toward the witness stand. A dog hopping toward a rabbit!

"Well?" asked Socks.

"Well what?"

"Are you offended?"

"No," said Peeps, a bit confused.

"You don't feel that I'm mocking you?"

"No. I think you look ridiculous, but—"

"But I'm not mocking you?"

"No."

"Triggering you? In any way?"

"No."

"Interesting." Socks walked back to his desk on all fours, then spun around quickly for his next question.

"Are you familiar with the work of a human psychologist named Jonny H?

"On student anti-fragility? Yes, he's quite well known."

"Can you explain Professor H's research to the jury?"

"Yes, of course. Actually, I have a PowerPoint in my office if you—"

"Thank you. No," Socks said. "Just tell us in your own words."

"Oh, uh, okay. Well, Jonny H claims that children, humans and animals, are anti-fragile. They play rough as children, fall down, get hurt, and get right back up and carry on. For example, the bones in mammalian bodies are designed to heal quickly, so even a serious break doesn't slow a creature down for too long. According to Jonny H, the natural anti-fragility of human and animal children is countermanded by hyper-controlling humans who coddle their children and pamper their pets. So, according to Professor H, the fragility of human and animal children is constructed. They believe they're fragile because they've been told as much for their whole lives, even though their biology and evolution prove the opposite."

This was brilliant testimony, Socks thought. Exactly what was needed to show that his use of the M-word really wasn't as bad as the cats had claimed. There was no need to ban that word, or any word, from the classroom. Human students, even feline students, could handle it.

Socks looked over to the jury box to see how the cats were tracking this testimony. His entire case hinged upon their understanding it. But instead of heads nodding up and down, signaling comprehension, he saw something else, something quite annoying. The cats weren't paying attention to the evidence at all. In fact, each and every one of the nine jurors was focused on a red dot that was dancing across the floor of the jury box, disappearing right in front of them, then reappearing behind them. Their eyes followed the dot; their paws batted it; their entire bodies pounced upon it, all to no avail—the red dot invariably escaped.

Some good-for-nothing cur has a laser pointer! Socks thought to himself as he quickly scanned the room. He determined that it must be coming from outside, but it was hard to see past the wall of muzzles and snouts pressed against the windows of the courtroom. When he was finally able to follow the red beam from the dot back to its source, he saw Lucifer, high in the elm tree, holding the laser in his beak and moving it just enough to keep the cats on their toes. The crow laughed out both sides of his mouth at all the havoc he was wreaking. The judge recognized the commotion and banged his gavel. Shouting for "order in the court," he directed Buck to close the shades. Once the cats settled down, Socks resumed his cross examination.

"Now, Professor Peeps. You were saying."

"I was just saying that Jonny H and his theory are controversial. Some even say wrong," Peeps said, in the most non-confrontational way one could imagine. Socks was still distracted by the cats and half worried that the laser pointer would reappear from some other angle. He barely listened as Peeps concluded his testimony.

"So, you see, Professor H's theory is very complicated and no one who cares about cats, or even human children, gives it much weight. Cats *are* fragile and if we as teachers don't acknowledge that and act accordingly, they'll end up being triggered into catatonia."

"No further questions," Socks said. "Wait. What?!"

"Professor Peeps, you may step down," the kangaroo said.

"Wait! Your honor. Redirect? Redirect!" the border collie shouted, but *locum tenens pro tempore* Judge Flash didn't know how to rule on this. He flipped through the pages of the Napoleonic code and the *Bürgerliches Gesetzbuch* but could not find a precedent. He looked up at the lone creature sitting in the court's gallery, the lupine president of Aesop College, Reynaldo Sourgrapes. The fox shook his head ever so slightly.

"No!" said Judge Flash all of the sudden. "I'm afraid you, uh, you can't redirect once you've ended your cross examination. You could redirect after the defense redirects. Do you want to redirect, Provost Hamhock?"

"Uh, no," Hamhock said.

And with that, Socks's best argument for student anti-fragility vanished into the ether, a victim of the rapid fading effect of spoken language. Gone. Socks would have to deal with it in his closing arguments, if he could. Meanwhile, the kangaroo looked again to the sole occupant of the gallery. The fox licked his lips, rubbed his stomach and mimed a chomping action with his teeth. The judge got the message.

"It's been a full morning," Jack Flash said. "Court is in recess until after lunch."

"COURT IS IN RECESS UNTIL 1PM," Buck shouted.

"Make it 1:30," said the kangaroo.

"COURT IS IN RECESS UNTIL 1:30," Buck said. He escorted the jury to an empty classroom on an upper floor of Reinvention Hall where they would be sequestered until the trial was over. Guinefort, in her preparations for the trial, had seen to it that an array of moist and dry cat food was put out for lunch. There was plenty of water (bottled, not from the tap), and each corner of the room had a freshly filled litterbox.

The judge retired to his chambers (the broom closet) to review his law books and eat a fresh-greens-on-toast sandwich that he had brought with him. Mrs. Pilfer hit the SAVE button on her laptop and left the room shaking her tiny rat hands to work out a cramp from all the typing. Sourgrapes and Hamhock exited through the crowd, through the main entrance of Reinvention Hall. It was good, the president thought, if the masses saw that he was the one providing justice for their grievances. Buck stayed behind to guard the courtroom, though he couldn't figure out what it needed guarding from—this was just his instinct.

Socks left through a side entrance to avoid the crowd. Remarkably, Argos and Jake, the mutt and the Bavarian fish hound, were waiting by the side door to greet him.

"What? ... How?"

"We know you, dog. And we've got your back."

The three dogs took the long way around the campus to the solitude of the faculty lounge (the old dog park). When they arrived, they found Toni the Chihuahua, who was crying.

"What's wrong?" Sock asked.

"Oh, don't be such a beagle!" Toni the Chihuahua said. "I'm worried for you."

"We're all worried," Argos said.

"What's your plan?" Jake asked. "Let us testify on your behalf."

"Or better yet," Toni the Chihuahua said, "let's get out of here. Skip town. Vamoose."

"No," Socks said. "To leave now would be admitting guilt and I've come too far for that."

"But anything could happen!" Argos said. "The jury could sentence you to death!"

"Let us testify as character witnesses," Jake offered again.

The two larger dogs began to lick the corners of Socks's mouth to show their respect for him. Toni the Chihuahua sat up on her haunches and looked at Socks with sad, pleading eyes.

"There must be some evidence that you can present that would prove your innocence," she said.

"There's no evidence," said Socks. "Evidence means facts and the only fact is that I did it, which isn't contested."

Socks then ranted about how student feelings were not evidence, even though hurt feelings seemed to be the linchpin of the prosecution's case.

"No," Socks continued. "This case would not be won with evidence, but with argumentation."

He then explained to his canine companions how he only had to prove a series of contingent arguments in order to win. First, the cats were not harmed. But if they were harmed, it wasn't as bad as they said it was. And if it was bad, they would get over it. More importantly, Socks had to show the jury the importance of academic freedom, show them how nothing else in this case mattered, and prove to them that no word should ever be banned from the classroom.

"I need time to think," Socks said. "Look, I appreciate what you're trying to do, but I need some time alone." Argos and Jake left, dejected. Toni the Chihuahua lingered, tried to offer comfort, but eventually she walked away, too, looking over her shoulder. Then, just as she walked through the dog park gate, she got an idea and rushed to catch up with Argos and Jake.

Socks sat in the middle of the faculty lounge, alone with his thoughts. Time always moves faster when one's life is on the line, he thought. He pulled himself together and returned to Reinvention Hall just as Buck was barking out "COURT IS NOW IN SESSION."

"Have you any further witnesses?" the judge asked the Provost.

"None, your honor. The prosecution rests."

"Call your first witness," the judge said to Socks.

The border collie sat up at his desk and stared into the distance. He looked at the jury, then at the Provost, then at the judge, then back at the jury, then at Buck, who squinted and smirked at him.

"The defense rests, your honor."

A bold move, Hamhock thought. What's he up to?

"Closing arguments?" the judge said.

"If it please the court," said Socks. He walked toward the jury, looked one more time back at the judge, the Provost, the bailiff, then he began.

"Mollies and Toms of the jury. Thank you for your consideration during this long and complex proceeding. It's ironic that your attention was diverted before lunch by the elusive red dot."

Socks smiled. Some of the cats looked away in embarrassment.

"As you know, a laser is meant to focus, but it can also distract. How is it that one thing can achieve two such different objectives? ... I suppose life is like that."

Socks fell into the peripatetic rhythm of his classroom lectures. The tone and cadence of his voice became hypnotic. *He* was now the red dot and the cats could not take their eyes off of him.

"Words can have more than one function, too," he said. They can be employed to hurt, but they also can and must be examined for understanding. We'll never understand the hurt in the world if we hide away the words used to cause that hurt. This is how it is with the M-word." He spun around to face the jury box and paused for effect.

"I've never denied saying that word in class ... but I assure you my intent was to make what the humans call a 'teachable moment.' Professor Peeps told you that my intent doesn't matter, only the impact of my actions. But the human philosophers distinguish between *use* and *mention*. All of today's witnesses said that I *used* the M-word. But that would mean that my intent was to harm them. I say that I didn't *use* the M-word, but only *mentioned* it, as part of a classroom discussion. Surely wise cats such as yourselves can see the distinction."

The dog makes some sense, some of the cats thought to themselves. They furrowed their brows and looked to one another for affirmation.

"Professor Peeps also claimed that cats are fragile, especially student cats. But Jonny H's theories assert that cats, indeed all creatures that walk on four legs, are anti-fragile."

Socks paused again and leaned in toward the jury box.

"Some of you will recall that Peeps was explaining the theories of Jonny H when the dreaded red dot appeared."

More embarrassed looks from the cats, but Socks just smiled and nodded, showing them that he understood and that he didn't fault them the distraction.

"Peeps said that no one gave any credence to Jonny H and his ideas. 'Cats are fragile,' he said over and over. 'Cats are fragile.' But this can't be right, and all of you know this. Especially as cats … you *know* this!"

They wanted to nod in agreement, but they weren't yet sure why.

"When a cat gets thrown from a roof," Socks asserted, "doesn't it always land on its feet?"

They looked at each other and nodded their approval. This had certainly been their experience and the replicable experience of every cat, as far as they knew.

"Don't we say that cats have nine lives?"

More nodding, with some deep purring thrown in.

"This is more than myth," Sock said. "We've all known cats or heard stories of cats who had 'something wrong' with them: a missing eye, a cut-off leg or a crooked tail, no hearing, even serious stuff like cancer. But those same cats still chased mice, still played with toys, still jumped in and out of empty boxes. They even attacked the red dot with the same vigor as so called 'normal' cats! Could there be better evidence of resilience and anti-fragility?"

Now the purring was audible throughout the room. Cats began rubbing up against furniture and two of them nuzzled their noses against Socks's chest.

"Let me close with a brief word about academic freedom. This is not the refuge of privileged, tenured professors. It's not just for dogs, but cats, too. *And* pigs *and* foxes *and* snakes *and* kangaroos *and and and*!

"If Aesop College doesn't commit to academic freedom, under the misguided assumption that it's protecting its students, then students will be denied the chance for intellectual growth, even moral growth. They won't have the tools they need to think out loud. And this won't serve anyone!"

There was silence for several seconds, then all of the animals in the quad, pressing their bodies and faces against the courtroom window, began to cheer, even those who had earlier been against Socks. Some of the feline jurors fell over onto their backs, rolled on the ground and batted at invisible insects. Jack Flash had to bang his gavel to restore order. Once the room was quiet again, Socks took his seat, and the judge gestured to Provost Hamhock to indicate that it was her turn for a closing argument. The pig took a breath and addressed the jury of cats directly.

"I warned you," Hamhock said. "I warned you that Professor Socks would make the worst argument into the best. Beyond agility courses and fly ball and catching disks, border collies are masters of rhetoric. And I'm afraid you've all been taken in by one of the best. Let's review the facts."

Hamhock took another long, slow breath.

"This has been a difficult time for our campus. Aesop College is a welcoming place, an inclusive place, a safe place. After all, the college motto is 'educating all.' But recent events have disrupted—"

As if on cue, upon hearing the word "disrupted," Jake, Argos, and Toni the Chihuahua burst into the courtroom, barking and yelping and running circles around the Provost as she tried to deliver her summation. After a moment of surprise, Buck jumped into action. He tried to disperse them, but with three targets it was difficult to pick one to pursue. Socks's three friends executed their plan.

Argos faced off with Buck to keep him at bay. Jake took hold of the Provost's leg and began to hump it to distract her from finishing her summation. Toni the Chihuahua leapt to the bench, where the judge was angrily banging his gavel. She wrestled the gavel from the kangaroo's hand and ran toward the jury box, causing the cats to scatter. Not knowing what else to do, or perhaps responding to instinct, Socks attempted to herd the cats back to the jury box. He was as surprised as anyone by what was happening, and he was happy to try and restore some semblance of order. Toni the Chihuahua dropped the gavel, stood up on her haunches, and addressed the feline jurors. Mrs. Pilfer—who in spite of all the madness around her had continued taking notes—calmly recorded the tiny dog's impassioned speech.

"Listen," Toni the Chihuahua implored, nearly out of breath. "You're turning Socks into a goat! That's what's really happening here! You're making him your goat!"

Toni the Chihuahua ran from cat to cat trying to make her point, which the cats found terribly uncomfortable. Her point also became more muddled, the more excited she got.

"They used to use a real goat," she cried. "It was sacrificed to purge all the sins, you know, of the whole pack. Okay, okay. There are sins at Aesop. The sins of species-ism. The sins of anti-cat-ism. But these aren't Socks's fault and you shouldn't punish *him* just because you want to punish *someone*. Don't make him the goatscape!"

"Scapegoat," Socks calmly corrected.

It was a noble attempt, but it fell apart as quickly as it began. Buck got the better of Argos, who ended up hiding under the judge's bench. Hamhock shook off Jake's attempts at dominance and pinned him to the floor under one of her expansive hams. Toni the Chihuahua found herself without any cover and she slowly backed away from the jury box and out of the room. Her two companions escaped their bonds and quickly followed. Meanwhile, the cats had once again scattered to every corner of the room, as the judge in this kangaroo court banged his gavel and cried for order.

"Well," Hamhock harrumphed. "I think that shows the level of disrespect the dogs have for this process."

"Objection!" Socks barked.

"Too late," Jack Flash said.

Hamhock agreed that her closing argument would not be necessary. The facts were the facts, and this final display demonstrated her most important point: that dogs had no respect for community standards. The judge banged his gavel one last time and court was adjourned.

The jury of cats was sequestered in the same room where they had eaten lunch. There was no food this time, though thankfully the litter boxes had been freshened up. There was much arguing and caterwauling back and forth. Four of the cats—Bella, Simba, Shadow, and Willow—were predisposed to find Socks guilty. So severe was their distaste for the M-word and all that it signified that there was no way they would acquit. Surprisingly, four of the cats had been listening to all of the testimony, in spite of the disruption with the laser pointer and the bedlam that had ended the trial. Chloe, Tigger Number Three, Smokey, and Romeo were able to consider Socks's closing arguments, in particular the part about the use/mention distinction. These four cats were convinced that Socks had not acted with malice aforethought, and therefore should be found not guilty.

This left the vote at 4 to 4, with a single juror undecided: Nala. The anti-Socks faction yowled and hissed and made a ruckus, but none of this convinced Nala. Attempts by the pro-acquittal faction were equally unsuccessful. After two hours of deliberation, the court reconvened, and the jury reported that they could not make a majority ruling. The judge polled the jurors one by one, but to no effect. He dismissed them with the thanks of the court and called a recess until he could determine a directed verdict. Judge *locum tenens pro tempore* Jack Flash withdrew to his chambers carrying his many law books with him. No one noticed the four black feet and bushy red tail that followed in behind him.

When he finally emerged from the broom closet, the kangaroo seemed jumpy. Would the animals in the Aesop community accept his verdict? he wondered. Would Socks mount an appeal? He struck the bench once with his gavel and began the heavily footnoted diatribe that was his ruling.

"This has been a difficult case," Flash said. "Academic freedom is allegedly at the core of this conflict, but equally important are the community standards that seem to have been violated. Cats have been injured. There is no doubt about that. That injury was caused by the utterance of a word, which Professor Socks spoke during his class. This is not contested, even by Socks himself. Socks had choices, but he chose to speak a word that violates community standards. Cats have been injured and redress must be made. Balance in the community must be restored."

For a mere graduate student, Jack Flash seemed almost eloquent. The listeners in the quad stood with their mouths agape. They could see what was coming, yet they were powerless to do anything about it.

"I therefore find Socks guilty of *ambitus*, as described in the *Corpus juris civilis*, the Roman law: 'using speech to impugn or humiliate another.' This was the effect of Socks's actions, whether or not it was his intent."

Animals watching from the quad began banging on the window. Some were in favor of the verdict, others opposed. There was such a huge kerfuffle that Buck went to the window and growled at the animals through the glass in an attempt to settle them down. Jack Flash banged his gavel until silence was restored, then continued.

"Usually, *ambitus* requires the death penalty," Flash said.

Gasp! went the crowd.

"In Roman times, the most common method of execution was the *poena cullei*, the punishment of the sack." Flash explained. The accused human, having been found guilty, was bound and placed in an ox-skin sack along with a snake, a dog, a monkey and a cockerel, then flung into a deep lake to be drowned. Unfortunately, not having an ox-skin sack, nor any desire to acquire one, this seemed to Jack Flash to be impractical at best, and at worst, a horrible fate for all the animals forced to participate.

"Can you imagine, what it must have been like?" he asked. "Imagine those panicking, terrified beasts, scratching and biting the accused as they tried to claw their way out of the sack, all the while drowning as they sank to the bottom of a lake." His description was so vivid that he himself shuddered at the thought.

"No," the judge said. "That won't do." He took a deep breath and turned several pages to another section of the Roman law.

"Instead, I propose exile. This was the verdict against the poet Ovid, who violated community standards with many of his poems. Since this case rests on the intersection of poetry and societal norms, this seems a just and fitting punishment."

The judge's ruling was at once brilliant and absurd, Socks thought. On the one paw, it was elegantly argued and based on legal precedent. On the other paw, what did ancient Roman law, a law of humans, have to do with the animal professors of Aesop College? Where in dog's name was the faculty handbook in all of this? Had the judge consulted that at all?

"The choice is yours," said Judge Jack Flash. "Exile or execution? I give you until noon tomorrow to decide."

CHAPTER 9

Buck took Socks into custody and locked him behind a pet safety gate in the old archives room in the basement of the library. He was not permitted to leave, but he was allowed visitors. During the course of the night, he received three.

His first visitor was President Sourgrapes, who appeared at dusk with a simple message: recant.

"I have the power to overturn the verdict," Sourgrapes said, "if you will only recant." The fox looked right into the border collie's heterochrome eyes.

"Renounce the Elliot poem and promise never to teach it again. Come clean about your anti-cat-ism. Decry the evils of the M-word and vow to strike it from your vocabulary."

Sourgrapes began to pace the edges of the archival room that was acting as a cell, looking pensively at the colorless walls as he spoke.

"Of course, you'll need to undergo some sensitivity training: a few more mandated listening sessions where the cats get to yowl and complain at you; some re-education lectures on the history of feline oppression; perhaps a few cat petting sessions, but only if and when the cats agree to be petted. And you'll have to write a real confession, not like that defensive diatribe you sent out last time. I could write it for you if you like and you can just sign it. Still not sure why the Provost never did that in the first place."

"And this would satisfy the aggrieved students?" Socks asked.

His first visitor was President Sourgrapes.

"Oh, not at first," Sourgrapes said, "and for some of them not ever. But they're only students, you know. They'll all graduate and move on and the animals will forget and soon no one will have any memory that this ever happened."

"But I'll know," Socks said.

"Yes, but you'll get back your life, such as it is."

"Only after performing this ritual penance?"

"Yes, I'm afraid so."

"Thank you for your visit," Socks said.

"Then we're on? You'll do it?"

"Thank you ... for your visit."

Long past midnight, Socks received his second visitor. It was Jake, his oldest friend.

"You've come to convince me to escape," Socks said.

"Yes," said Jake. "It would be easier for me to convince the judge, that imbecile kangaroo, that tool of our cunning president, that he should sentence you to a lifetime of luxurious dinners for the service you've rendered the academy. Instead, I'm here, trying to convince *you* to run away, right now, to save your own life. I'll take care of Buck. You just run and run and run and don't look back."

"I'm not upset by how this has played out," Socks said. "I always expected a guilty verdict from a jury comprised entirely of cats. It's amazing that they split their votes. I thought the majority against me would have been bigger. Then to get a hung jury and have Flash rule for the death penalty, with exile as a concession! Amazing."

"Stand not amazed, my friend. The Prince will doom thee death, if thou art taken. So, get thee to a nunnery, or a cathouse, or some other dog-forsaken place that ain't here! The judge's only offer is a one-way ticket across the rainbow bridge!"

"Please don't mash up the Bard like that. You know how irritating I find it."

Jake shrugged.

"Besides," Socks asked, "Why worry about death? Death is either something or it's nothing. If it's something, it can't be more annoying than wandering in exile, forced to confront more of the world's ignorance, or changing the very nature of who I am just to get along and avoid conflict. And if death is nothing, then so what?"

"O bloody hell! You're as stubborn as an English bulldog!"

"Avoiding death would be easy," Socks said. "Avoiding unrighteousness, as a human philosopher once said, is much more difficult. For 'unrighteousness runs faster than death,' and the fastest greyhound is no match for it."

Defeated in his errand, Jake lay down in front of his friend and faced the wall of the cell. Socks settled beside him and rested his head on his friend's shoulder. The two lay still, not sleeping, but in each other's company. It was the middle of the night when the red Bavarian fish hound rose to leave. The two dogs looked at each other for the last time.

"What can I do?" Jake asked. "What can I *do*?"

"Forget it, Jake. It's Aesop College."

He left without looking back.

Socks's third visitor came at dawn and brought the biggest surprise. It was Robespierre, the striped tabby who had been his most vocal critic.

"I've been waiting for you," Socks said.

"Oh, please," said Robespierre rolling his cat eyes.

"Have you forgotten my lecture on the *scène à faire* in the well-made play?"

"The obligatory scene!" said Robespierre. "The scene that must be witnessed by the audience and not reported by a messenger as off-stage action. The scene in which the hero and the villain resolve their conflict with the one killing the other."

"Very good."

"So, who am I?" asked Robespierre "And who are you? The hero or the villain?"

"These are questions of interpretation," the professor told his student. Even as he approached death, Socks would not give the answers away. Robespierre squinted his eyes and involuntarily arched his back.

"I wasn't gunning for your job, you know. Even now, I think it's better if you kept teaching. You're not a villain, but you don't have to be a prick either." Socks smiled at him but did not respond.

"If only you could actually listen to the students whom you think you're lifting up with your teaching, instead of doubling down on all this academic freedom crap, which you and I both know doesn't come anywhere close to justifying your behavior. You're lucky that academic freedom is such a sexy topic these days 'cause it's a lot easier to hide behind a 'concept' than face the fact that, intentional or not, you hurt your students … You *hurt* your *students*." Robespierre took a moment to let that sink in, then finished.

"I admired you as a teacher, Socks. Now I only see you as a disappointment. You've become a defensive, prideful person who thinks he's in too deep to just admit he fucked up. It must be hard to look in the mirror and come to terms with all the wrong you've done. I hope you can figure that out someday."

Socks looked at Robespierre and smiled broadly, feeling the love that only a teacher can feel for his student. Neither of them would kill the other in this obligatory scene, he thought, as unsatisfying as that might be for the audience of this ill-made play.

"I know you're a fan of the 'hero's journey,'" Socks said to Robespierre. "An acolyte of Campbell's monomyth, hoping for revelation, transformation, and atonement in our story." He looked at Buck guarding the door. "But I'm afraid you're going to be disappointed. I just don't feel much in the mood for it."

"Then your story's a tragedy," said Robespierre. "You *have* had a revelation. Admit it or don't. But you've chosen not to change or atone. It didn't have to be this way. Tragic."

"Thank you for your visit," Socks said, still smiling.

The striped tabby had hoped for more. No final round of debate? he wondered. No point-counterpoint for the road? Nothing? But that was it. Thank you for your visit. The cat drew several figure eights on the floor as he left the room, didn't leave the room, left the room, wound back around, and then finally left for good.

At noon, Provost Hamhock and Jack Flash arrived at Socks's cell.

"Have you chosen?" the kangaroo asked solemnly.

"I chose long ago to lead the poet's life, though in truth I'm more a teacher of poetry than a true poet."

Socks's eyes took on a faraway look. If I'd been a guard dog, like Buck, he thought, I would have stood my post with no thought of danger or impending death. To leave my post would have been the greatest dishonor. But I'm not a guard dog. I'm a teacher whose only post has been to teach the truth as I understood it. If I gave up teaching the truth just because a smidgeon of danger or a smattering of death appeared at my door ... well, that would be shameful. He looked at the kangaroo, then looked one last time directly into the Provost's eyes.

"I choose death," he said.

And that was the end of Socks.

The agility champion turned college professor requested death by an overdose of catnip tea. He loved the irony of it— dying slowly and blissfully. Socks's execution was not a public affair. Such barbaric rituals were too human to suit the tastes of the animals at Aesop College. In an isolated wood, near a river that ran behind the campus, three animals attended the execution as witnesses: Jack Flash, in his last official act as judge, Provost Hamhock, representing the administration, and Toni the Chihuahua, who had coerced Socks into letting her come. Hamhock poured about a gallon of catnip tea into a large, metal dog bowl.

"This didn't have to end like this," said the Provost.

"Better to die for one's beliefs than to sit around waiting for the butcher," said Socks.

Your wit cuts deep, the Provost thought.

Those were Socks's final words and his last ticks on earth. He lapped up the catnip tea until the bowl was shiny and dry, had a brief fit of giggling, then fell into the long sleep. No modern-day Jacques Louis David captured on canvas that dramatic moment when Socks drank his final dram, when his *animus* left his animal body. Except for this modest chronicle, the border collie faded from all animal and human memory.

Toni the Chihuahua threw herself on Socks's limp body and began to sob. Flash reached out a hand to comfort her, but Hamhock pulled him back. The pig and the kangaroo left the tiny dog alone in the forest to mourn her friend's death. They could still hear her cries in the distance when they arrived back on campus.

Toni the Chihuahua sat next to Socks for what seemed like hours. Suddenly, she saw a tremor in Socks's front paws, a slight kicking of his back legs, as if he were chasing rabbits in his sleep. The dog's eyes blinked, then squinted, then popped wide open. He tried to stand but wobbled horribly.

"Well, this can't be the rainbow bridge," Socks said.

"You don't believe in that anyway," replied Toni the Chihuahua.

"What happened? Am I not dead?"

"You're about as sharp as a bag full of wet gerbils," Toni said. "Nobody dies from catnip!"

"Huh?"

"You are going to have one helluva hangover, though."

Socks fumbled back to a prone position as Toni the Chihuahua, chemistry professor, explained.

"Catnip, or catmint, *nepeta cataria,* as we chemists say, was once used by humans as a cure for colds, colic, and, of all things, hemorrhoids. The active ingredient, the stuff that makes the cats go nuts, is called nepetalactone, which researchers have shown affects even big cats, like lions and tigers. Cat *thyme*, on the other paw, is similar to catnip, but it's actually very addictive. In uncontrolled experiments, cats have been known to sniff it in until they get nose bleeds and destroy their olfactory glands. However, in the entire history of catnip, there have only been three deaths attributed to overdose, but most scientists contest these reports." *Nepeta cataria* is neither addictive nor harmful, and it certainly can't kill you."

Socks looked at her with his mouth open.

"You knew all along," he said.

"Hello. My name is Toni. I'm a bitch. And a professor. And a *chemist.*"

Unsuccessful at becoming a martyr for the cause of academic freedom, Socks was left to ponder his other options. Before his pondering had gotten very far, Jake and Argos showed up in the forest clearing. Socks appeared confused.

"She told us," said Argos.

"She told us," said Jake.

Socks half smiled, but his head still felt like a raccoon fighting its way out of a Havahart live animal trap. Toni the Chihuahua began walking and motioned for the other dogs to follow. She led them out of the forest in the opposite direction from Aesop. After several hours walking in silence, Toni the Chihuahua turned to Socks.

"Think you'll ever teach again?"

Socks shrugged, but he started imagining what it might be like. Could he find students who would want to work with him? What books might they read together? What ideas could they talk about? His canine friends soon joined in this reverie and they talked and walked into the night. Aesop became a dot on the horizon. They never looked back.

Life at Aesop College went on, at least for a while.

The campus lost its reputation as a first-rate, institution of animal higher education. The animal professors who already taught there lived in fear of making a mistake in the classroom and possibly suffering the same fate as their "deceased" colleague. The free flow of animal ideas was stifled. Lectures became trite and outdated repetitions of the same old stuff. In such a climate, it was nearly impossible to attract new professors.

The cats and other students, who believed the purpose of school was to pamper them, ended up never learning anything. This wasn't just a detriment to their intellectual lives, but to their daily lives as well. For instance, because cats no longer learned basic self-defense, more cats were run over by trucks when crossing the street. Instinct could only take them so far. Luckily, cats really are anti-fragile and most of them were able to get right up after an accident and cross the street again. Some of them even learned enough to cross without getting hit a second time.

Worst of all, the Aesop cats believed they had scored a victory by removing Socks from the classroom. The college administrators and other elders had given in to their demands so quickly that the cats believed they were "special" and that all animals should kowtow to their "specialness"— though they always pointed out that the word "kowtow" was in no way meant as in insult to cows. The cats were often surprised when some uneducated dog (a true anti-cat-ite) attacked them physically, all the while laughing at their assertions of "status" and "power differentials." Some cats were so completely incapable of defending themselves, either physically or intellectually, that they were ripped to shreds, both rhetorically and literally.

Aesop College never did solve its retention problem. As more and more kittens "dropped out," President Reynaldo Sourgrapes got fatter and fatter. None of the animals noticed. No fingerprints. Eventually, animal parents stopped sending their young to Aesop, believing that education in the wild would be better than anything the school had to offer.

Aesop College grew more and more empty and less and less relevant. One day, J. "Dusty" Adams, former president of McDonald College (Aesop's predecessor), arrived at the school in a dark-blue minivan. Adams had become a real estate speculator, a vocation much more suited to his skill set. He removed a large sign that was tied to the roof of the minivan and installed it on the edge of campus. The sign read as follows:

Future home of

AESOP'S CONDOMINIUMS

Fabulist living for the discriminating pet owner!

Adams financed the building of the condos, which served neither human students hoping to reinvent the world nor animal students hoping to evolve as a species. Now, when animals walked across the campus, they found themselves on leashes. Only the squirrels were free to roam as they wished.

When the tides of "bark out" culture turned, Gullinburst Hamhock, once Provost at Aesop College, was forced to resign in shame. It never looked good when the so-called leader of the faculty promoted the demise of academic freedom. Hamhock never worked in higher education again. Instead, she lived in a small backroom in the home of her former "owner," Liliana Carnevale. Lili, once a professional vegan, now managed a chain of barbecue joints. Her husband, Bob Metzger, was a butcher. Hamhock tutored the Metzger-Carnevale children in basic math: percentages, weights and measures, and what her human charges called "*gozintas*," as in "3 *gozinta* 18 six times" and "a dozen *gozinta* a gross twelve times." These were the building blocks of calculation necessary for successful careers in the food service industry.

Gone were the days when Hamhock rehearsed the calculus in Newton's *Principia Mathematica*. Gone was the life of the mind that had once fed Hamhock's soul—though she was careful never to call it "soul food." Aside from working far below her intellectual capacity, she spent most of her time making sure the butcher's children stayed happy and that nothing in her pedagogy upset them. She imagined dire consequences if that ever happened. As the old saying went: "Pigs are like saints, more honored when dead than alive."

On one of her medium rare days off, Hamhock visited the Aesop Condominiums. She wandered into Reinvention Hall, now a party room for the condo residents.

All the faculty meetings I led here, she reminisced. The trial. That was a time when animals rose above their stations and stood for something. Some animals even died for their beliefs. As she left the building, she looked back and saw the name still carved in stone above the door. The bright red paint had faded from some of the letters, leaving behind an unintended but apt commentary.

RE INVENTION

Hamhock rolled her eyes, shook her head, and waddled off the old McDonald campus for the last time.

THE END

Acknowledgements

Thanks to Randall Davidson for giving me the idea for this book. Thanks to beta readers Julie Bolton, Lisa Channer, Jan Jackson, and Patrick Romey. Thanks to Peter Schulz of Theran Press for his encouragement. Thanks to the many Facebook friends who gave their input on the cover, especially Bill Caraher who helped with the fonts. Thanks to Maria Jette for her excellent proofreading skills, and for suggesting that the book be illustrated. Finally, thanks to Watercolorcirp for creating those wonderful illustrations.

The body text of this book
is set in Baskerville, as in
"Hound of the —s."